The GENESIS MESSAGE

A New Look at the Old Stories

Harvey A. Smit

CRC Publications
Grand Rapids, Michigan

Reformed Church Press
New York, New York

Cover art © Clint Hansen

The Scripture quotations in this publication are from the HOLY BIBLE, NEW INTERNATIONAL VERSION, © 1973, 1978, 1984, International Bible Society. Used by permission of Zondervan Bible Publishers.

The Genesis Message: A New Look at the Old Stories, © 1999 by CRC Publications, 2850 Kalamazoo Avenue SE, Grand Rapids, MI 49560.

All rights reserved. With the exception of brief excerpts for review purposes, no part of this book may be reproduced in any manner whatsoever without written permission from the publisher.

Printed in the United States of America on recycled paper. ✪

Library of Congress Cataloging-in-Publication Data
Smit, Harvey A. (Harvey Albert), 1928-1998
　　The Genesis message : a new look at the old stories / Harvey A. Smit.
　　p.　　cm.
　　ISBN 1-56212-416-1
　　1. Bible.　O.T.　Genesis—Study and teaching.　I. Title.
　BS1235.5.S63　1999
　22'.11'0071—dc21　　　　　　　　　　　　　　　99-38829
　　　　　　　　　　　　　　　　　　　　　　　　　CIP

10 9 8 7 6 5 4 3 2 1

Contents

Introduction			7
Chapter 1	The Creation Story	Genesis 1:1-19	9
Chapter 2	Caretakers of Creation	Genesis 1:20-2:4a	13
Chapter 3	Partners	Genesis 2:4b-2:25	17
Chapter 4	The Fall	Genesis 3	21
Chapter 5	Cain and Abel	Genesis 4:1-17	25
Chapter 6	The Flood	Genesis 6:5-7:24	29
Chapter 7	Rainbows	Genesis 8:1-9:17	33
Chapter 8	Babel	Genesis 11:1-9	37
Chapter 9	God's Call to Abram	Genesis 11:27-12:9	41
Chapter 10	Hagar and Ishmael	Genesis 16	45
Chapter 11	Meeting at Mamre	Genesis 18:1-15	49
Chapter 12	A Challenge to God's Justice	Genesis 18:16-33	53
Chapter 13	Abraham Tested	Genesis 22:1-19	57
Chapter 14	A Wife for Isaac	Genesis 24	61
Chapter 15	Struggle for the Blessing	Genesis 25:19-34; 27	65
Chapter 16	God Blesses Jacob	Genesis 29:14b-30:43	69
Chapter 17	The Brothers Meet	Genesis 32-33	73
Chapter 18	Joseph the Dreamer	Genesis 37	77
Chapter 19	Joseph the Slave	Genesis 39; 41:1-46	81
Chapter 20	Joseph and His Brothers	Genesis 42; 44:18-45:15	85

A Tribute

Harvey A. Smit served as editor in chief of the Education, Worship, and Evangelism department of CRC Publications from 1977 to 1997. Though fighting cancer, he found time during his short "retirement" to work on *The Genesis Message* and on a number of other projects. Harvey passed away on September 17, 1998. He was seventy years old.

We who were privileged to work with Harv at CRC Publications remember him as a man who dearly loved the church he served so well. We remember him as a wise and deeply thoughtful colleague and friend. We remember him as an insightful theologian and a creative writer who made familiar Bible stories as fresh as if we were reading them for the first time. We remember him as a man of gentle humor and graceful humility.

For these and for so many more things that are beyond words, we will always cherish and honor the memory of this man of God.

The EWE Staff

Introduction

The Bible is the greatest "how-to" book ever written. Other books may tell you how to get rich quick, how to lose thirty pounds, or how to save your marriage. The Bible tells you something far more important. It's an instruction book on how to find peace with God and how to be forgiven for everything you've done wrong—or, simply, how to be saved.

Most people in our day realize this is what the Bible is about. Some of them may get a copy and start to read it because they want to know how to be saved. But when they open that book, they find that it's as if it had been written in old English or in some technical jargon they don't fully understand. True, the Bible contains lots of interesting stories about people being slaves, fighting wars, or being miraculously healed. It also contains some wonderful prayers to God, stories about the church, and teachings on how people should live with each other. But the Bible doesn't seem to have the simple how-to instructions that modern people have come to expect. It doesn't outline ten steps to find peace with God or the seven things you must do to have your sins forgiven. And a lot of it just plain doesn't make sense to people. What does Abraham leaving his hometown and heading out with his family to some foreign territory have to do with our getting to know God? What does Jesus arguing with the Pharisees about whether it's okay to heal on the Sabbath Day have to do with my salvation? And why does Paul get all bent out of shape because some Jewish Christians think Gentiles also should be circumcised?

Even people who have been Christians for a long time have trouble understanding many parts of the Bible. They've had a lot of instruction on reading the Bible—in a sense that's what sermons provide—but they still don't know what questions to ask, how to identify underlying themes and ideas, and how to understand any one part of the Bible in terms of the teaching of the entire book.

If you're looking for instructions on how to read the Bible, there are some very good books available. One of the best is Gordon D. Fee & Douglas Stuart's work *How to Read the Bible for All Its Worth*. Several Jewish authors have written outstanding guides to reading the Old Testament, like

Robert Alter's *The World of Biblical Literature*. But most of these can get pretty technical and they tend to *talk about* reading the Bible rather than actually helping people to *practice* reading it with understanding.

The Genesis Message: A New Look at the Old Stories concentrates on the narratives—on the stories the Bible tells. Stories make up a little more than half of the entire Bible. This study goes through the stories in Genesis in a fairly systematic way. It points out some of the things that are happening in each story, why it's being told in this specific way, and what truths it's trying to teach. It also asks a few questions for you to think about in relation to each particular story. This study will take you on a guided walk through Genesis and, we hope, enable you to take a new look at its treasure of well-known and much-loved stories.

The Genesis Message: A New Look at the Old Stories is meant first of all for personal use. Ideally, you'll read through the recommended Scripture passage once, slowly and thoughtfully, and then read the text, which will direct you to reread certain sections of the Scripture passage. As you are doing that, you might think about the questions that are placed in the right-hand margin; you may wish to keep a journal, writing down your thoughts regarding these questions and any other questions that might occur to you. Finally, if you have time, read through the passage one more time, thinking about the message it has for you.

This study can be very easily adapted for small group use. Have someone, or several people, read the passage aloud. Then read the text in sections, pausing to discuss what is being said and to talk about the questions or comments in the right-hand margins. Depending on the length of time your group meets, you can take several of the suggested passages, or you might become so involved in discussion of a particular passage that it will take all of your group's time just to cover that one.

However you use this book, remember that its purpose is to help you in your own reading and understanding of the Bible. It should turn you again and again to the actual biblical text, helping you to read it more thoughtfully and carefully. As you do this, the Genesis stories will help you to learn more about God's ways of dealing with us. The Bible is God's how-to book. It is the Word of Life. Only from it can we learn the God-given way of salvation and how we can live a life that is pleasing to our Lord.

Harvey A. Smit

CHAPTER 1

THE CREATION STORY
Genesis 1:1-19

"In the beginning . . ." This opening phrase gives the entire book its name—*Genesis,* Greek for *beginnings.* Glance through the book and you realize that it traces the beginnings not only of the world but also of humanity and of the separate people called out by the Lord. The only other book in the Bible that starts with the same words, the gospel of John, traces the beginnings of Jesus' ministry and the new people of God.

"In the beginning God . . ." These words signal that you won't find scientific analysis of evidence here. Rather, you find a call to faith. What follows is not a Bible story in the traditional sense but a proclamation of the mighty and majestic creative work of God.

"In the beginning God created the heavens and the earth." That's the action you'll find described from here to the echoing conclusion of this passage (2:4a). This is a flat statement, not a subject for debate. It tells you that what follows will not be a mythological view that assumes that the real action is among the gods and that creation itself has no value. Nor is it a scientific view that looks only to the world itself and the mysteries it contains. Rather, it gives us a covenantal view that locates creation's ultimate meaning and value in the purposes of its Creator.

> **Why are beginnings important? Do they determine everything that follows? What about your own beginnings?**

> **What is the popular scientific view on how the world began? How does this view square with the opening sentence of Genesis 1?**

Order out of Chaos

Does Genesis present us with two contrary views of creation, the first depicting God creating the universe out of nothing at all and the second showing God ordering what was already there? Or do you think these two views can be reconciled?

How did God create? The accepted Christian teaching is that the Creator called the world into being out of nothing (based on Rom. 4:17 and Heb. 11:3). But the Genesis passage really emphasizes that God created by bringing order to what was originally dark and chaotic, "formless and empty" (v. 2). Out of a terrifying chaos, like a wild sea at night, God fashioned a suitable habitat for the human race (Isa. 45:18).

Read further in Genesis and you will find a pervasive emphasis on the order of creation. In fact, God creates by a very ordered process—giving a command, seeing what was commanded happen, making a judgment about this new thing, naming it, and, in some cases, blessing it. Each episode is followed by the words, "and there was evening and there was morning—the first (second, third . . .) day." That pattern repeated throughout the creation process intends to give the reader a sense of the irresistible flow of God's creative activity and of our Creator's complete control of every aspect.

What does it mean that the Spirit (wind) of God was hovering over the waters? Is this a pre-creative presence of God above the waters of chaos?

Creation involves eight divine acts occurring over six days. In the first act God says, "Let there be light" (v. 3). Notice that this is no magical word—it's an intelligible one. Still, it's remarkable that God creates by speaking! According to the Bible this is the chosen divine way of acting in our world. Consider the words spoken to Abraham (Gen. 12:1), to Moses (Ex. 3:4ff.), to Elijah, to the rest of the prophets (1 Kings 17:2), and finally to Jesus, the Word of God become flesh (John 1:14). Why does God use speech? Perhaps because speech permits an answer. It invites a response. As we will see in the later part of the creation story, human beings are designed to give such a response.

If you didn't know the Genesis account and you were asked to write the story of creation, where would you begin? With the stars, perhaps? Or with a cosmic event? Explain your choice.

You may wonder how it was possible to have light before the heavenly bodies were created. But this account doesn't begin with a scientific view of the stars and planets as sources of light. It starts with our human experience of day following night. By starting with that, Genesis creates a time frame in which the rest of creation can occur. Next comes a spatial frame when God divides the waters above (that come as rain through holes in the sky) from the waters below (the sea and the springs that bubble up from the ground). Then, on day three, God creates the dry ground and the seas, making places in which animals and humans can live.

Notice that in each case, God creates by separating (vv. 4, 7, 9). In other words, the Creator takes what is chaotic (night, the waters, and the sea) and gives it an ordered place.

It is not destroyed but rather incorporated into the pattern of creation. The divine naming is a final act of dominion. Naming asserts control and rule.

ON THE THIRD AND THE FOURTH DAYS

After these three initial creative acts, God judges his handiwork to be good (vv. 4, 10). This is not a moral judgment, but rather a statement about the beauty and perfection of what has been made. Don't take it as a sort of divine self-congratulation either. Rather, read it as an invitation to the reader to praise the Creator. The sheer goodness of creation, its wondrous excellence, should make us sing praise to God.

In the fourth creative act (vv. 11-12), instead of the usual "Let there be . . . ," God says, "Let the land produce vegetation. . . ." Given God's divine permission, the land itself brings forth—not in a wild, accidental way but in an ordered process. Each brings forth "according to their kind."

Does the account present some idea of "mother earth" here? Or does it just reflect the farmer's experience?

On the fourth day, in the fifth creative act, God makes the sun, moon, and stars. To the scientific mind that order seems odd. The day and night have already been separated on the first day, and now, finally, we get the sun and moon "to govern the day and the night and to separate light from darkness" (v. 18). Why place them here in the creative process? It's because the author of this account is now moving on to describe the origin of living creatures. To people of that time the heavenly bodies fit in that category; most considered them gods, beings to be worshiped.

The biblical account asserts pointedly that these lights are made and set in place by God. They are created objects with specific functions assigned by the Creator—to serve as signs and to govern the day and the night. So the author refutes any idea that these lights are divine.

In this account, there is only one Divine Being. God creates by speaking a word and, without pause or intermediary steps, what God says happens. There is majesty in the creative acts, as God says, sees, names, and judges. In this account there is no blind, evolutionary groping toward our present world. God speaks and it is so. Let all praise the Creator.

What image of God do you gain from this account? Is it incomplete without the rest of the creation story?

CHAPTER 2

CARETAKERS OF CREATION
Genesis 1:20-2:4a

The latter half of the creation story culminates in three great divine acts: the creation of living fish and birds, land animals, and human beings. The story ends in a proclamation of divine rest. As nothing earlier has done, the creation of humankind and the day of rest disclose the divine purpose in all this creative activity.

On the fifth day and sixth day God creates the creatures who will inhabit the newly created dwelling place. Notice the close parallels between the making of water creatures, birds, and land animals. All are created "according to their kind" (vv. 21, 24-25). Although there are swarms of new creatures, these don't appear in an unordered chaos. Each has its place in the created pattern. And each is judged by the Creator to be good (vv. 21, 25).

> **How does this creation ordering compare with the scientific orders and species?**

Notice also that the order in which these creatures are made matches the order in which their habitats were formed. The separation of the waters to form the sky preceded the forming of the dry land. So water animals and birds precede land animals. It all follows a strict pattern.

On the fifth day, a new element enters the picture—a divine blessing. This benediction is extended to water and air creatures and also to human beings (vv. 22, 28). Why this blessing? Perhaps because these creatures have the breath of

> **Why is there no blessing on land animals? Is it because they are produced by the land (1:24) and therefore share in its fertility? Or are they included in the blessing on humankind (v. 28)?**

life which comes directly from God (see Gen. 2:7). That tie to divine life was not present in earlier creation. The blessing gives the power to reproduce, to "be fruitful and increase" (1:22, 28).

THE CREATION OF HUMANS

What picture does his divine "us" form in your mind? Of a king? A boss? Head of a family? Or a caretaker?

With the creation of human beings, the pattern followed earlier is broken. God no longer just says, "Let there be...." Instead, God says, "Let us make man...." (1:26). That indicates a separate divine decision. The divine "us" has been variously explained as a reference to the Trinity, to a divine court with whom God confers, or to the Hebrew plural of deliberation. We find support for the last explanation elsewhere in Scripture. In Genesis 11:7 and in other passages, God uses a similar deliberative plural to indicate careful thought before deciding to do a new thing. However we understand the "us," it tells us that something very important is about to happen—the creation of human beings.

Man (the Hebrew word is *adam*, meaning *humankind*) is formed in the divine image and likeness (1:26). In Christian history there has been a strenuous debate about what *image* means in this context. Ideas range from certain spiritual qualities to bodily shape. But aside from strongly prohibiting the making of any images of God (Ex.20:4) and speaking of Jesus as "the image of the invisible God" (Col. 1:15), the rest of the Bible says almost nothing about this divine likeness.

How do you think of human "rule"? Is it tyranny, permitting abuse? A shepherd's control over his sheep? Relate this to Jesus' words to his disciples in Mark 10:43-44.

What does "image of God" mean? Evidently it's not some special quality, but something rooted in our relationship to God. Verse 26 goes on to say that humankind is to rule over the fish, the birds, and all the creatures that move along the ground. Ancient kings would erect images of themselves in distant cities to represent their ruling presence. So God evidently places humankind to act as his stewards on the earth.

Why are humans at the top of the created order? Because of an evolutionary accident? Bigger brains? A divinely given right to rule? The ability to speak to God?

But there may be another aspect to this image. God never speaks directly to the fish, birds, or other animals. God speaks directly only to humans (1:28-30). God says "you" when addressing humankind. That shows a unique relationship in which the rest of creation does not share. It also shows a unique ability and freedom to respond to God. We are invited into a covenantal relationship with God.

Notice that *adam* is created both male and female (1:27). That seems to say that the division into two sexes is part of creation, not of God. It also says that sexuality is part of the created order, not of the fall. It is included in all that God proclaims to be good. Notice that in 1:26-28 there seems to be an odd combination of singular and plural in referring to humans. It's as if God is sometimes talking to single entities and at other times to humans in community.

The Day of Rest

After pronouncing everything "very good" (1:31), "on the seventh day God rested [the Hebrew word *shabat* means *ceased*] from all his work" (2:2). That does not mean that, tired by all the creative work, God took time off. Rather, the day of rest is a divine sign that the work of creation is finished. It's complete! No more needs to be added. God signals that he will not interfere with this created order. It is very good as it is. Of course, God continues to maintain it and give it life, but there will be no more of these gigantic creative acts.

The day of rest divides the week into regular time and holy time, into time for work and time for rest (the Sabbath). God institutes a basic polarity here that is meant to be present in all of creation. The seventh day is "made holy" (2:3). This lays the basis for the later commandment, "Remember the Sabbath day by keeping it holy" (Ex. 20:8).

The day of rest also tells us that humanity is not the end and goal of creation. Everything begins and ends with God. We say both "In the beginning God created . . ." and in the end "God rested." By this day of rest, creation is made part of God's overall plan in history. The divine work of creation sets the stage for the divine work of salvation that culminates in the Lord Jesus Christ. And this will all lead to the time when "The kingdom of the world has become the kingdom of our Lord and of his Christ, and he will reign for ever and ever" (Rev. 11:15).

What impression of God do you get from this entire creation process? Of a tyrant? Of a distant craftsman? Of one who delights in what has been made? Or of a God eager to enter into covenant with his creatures?

CHAPTER 3

PARTNERS
Genesis 2:4b-2:25

Read the first verses of this account and you may wonder what we have here: a second creation story, a detailed account of the creation of humankind, or neither?

To answer that question, first recognize that the chapter divisions and the headings given to the various sections in our versions of the Bible are not part of the original text. The chapter divisions were added by ancient editors to aid in public readings. The section headings are interpretations by modern editors. You don't need to take either as authoritative.

Now do a quick scan of the text from Genesis 2:4b to the end of chapter 3. You should sense here a single, unified story. Notice the unusual designation, "the Lord God," used throughout this story but not in earlier or later chapters. And notice all the themes introduced in the first part and developed in the second (living in and being expelled from the Garden, receiving and disobeying the command not to eat of a certain tree, and so on). If our text is the first part of a single story, what is that story trying to say to us?

Imagine the author looking at his world with its mix of good and bad, of joy and suffering, of freedom and bondage, and asking how all this came to be. The answer, he tells us, lies in humankind's initial relationship to God. Everything starts well, but then it goes bad. This text relates the good beginning.

When biblical accounts are referred to as "stories," does that make them sound like fiction? Like something for children only? Or does it make you think of oral accounts passed on from one generation to another and then written down? If the latter, when did the guiding of God's Spirit (2 Tim. 3:16; 2 Pet. 1:20) come? At the oral stage? Only at the writing stage?

A Living Being

> If you reject the Greek notion of a naturally immortal soul, how do you account for the Christian hope of eternal life? Is immortality a given or is it solely a divine gift (see Mark 10:30; 1 Cor. 15:53)?

Verses 5 and 6 give us the setting of the creation of humanity. God makes the first human being (Adam) out of the dust of the ground (*adamah*). So humanity remains tied to the ground from which they came and to which they will return (Ps. 90:3). Notice the image here of God hunkering down like a potter forming a pot, shaping this human form with his own hands (Job 10:8-9). Then God breathes into this piece of clay the breath of life, making it a living being. There is nothing here of the Greek myth of a naturally immortal soul being imprisoned in a mortal body. A human being is a unity.

In verse 8 the image of the divine potter is replaced by one of the divine planter of a garden. The location of this garden, in Eden at the confluence of four rivers, means little to us today. We don't know what it might have meant to earlier readers.

> The man is put to work in the garden. Do you think of work as a blessing or a curse? In this story it seems to be a blessing that becomes a curse (3:17-19). What is it for you today?

This pleasing and fruitful garden is evidently intended for God's enjoyment (3:8) and as a living place for humankind. The man is placed here, given the task of taking care of it, and permitted to eat freely of all its fruit. This is a wonderfully gracious act of God. Most masters would let a gardener eat from one or two poor trees. God places only one limitation on this great privilege. Of the tree of the knowledge of good and evil (in the Hebrew this is not moral knowledge but the polarities of existence) the man may not eat, on pain of death.

The Creation of Eve

With verse 18 comes something quite unexpected and new to the creation. God proclaims something in the creation is "not good." Humankind is evidently incomplete. The man lacks a suitable helper, someone who will complement him and permit him to live in community.

> What do you understand by "suitable helper"? A "go-fer"? A partner? A companion? What difference might it make that God is called our "help" in Psalm 54:4?

God decides to provide this helper, but doesn't do so immediately. First, the man must experience his own lack and discover his own need. And this takes place through his naming all the animals, both tame and wild beasts and birds. This naming is an exercise of the "rule" given earlier (1:26). By naming each animal, the man assigns it a place in his world. This is human ordering, a shadow of the divine ordering in the creation process.

While the man names the animals, it becomes obvious that there is no suitable helper for him. So God sets out to provide one. First God puts the man to sleep. This should not be understood as some primitive notion of an anesthetic before an operation. It may indicate that the man is not permitted to see the process by which God creates the woman, that there is a mystery here. The text says that God took "part of the man's side" to make a woman. The idea seems to be that woman is a separate but not a wholly "other" being from man. They belong side by side.

Notice the jubilant poetic words with which the man greets the woman. There is a profound recognition that this new person is "bone of my bones and flesh of my flesh" (v. 23). The man joyfully welcomes this life partner who completes him and permits him to live in community.

Verse 24 interrupts the flow of the story. The author informs us that this deep relationship between the man and the woman is the reason underlying the institution of marriage and the forming of new families. "Becoming one flesh" means more than a sexual union. It refers to becoming a new, complete, personal community.

Before the story goes on to tell about the disintegration of the glory of *Paradise* (the Persian word for *garden*), it pictures this husband and wife as both naked and unashamed. Why aren't they ashamed? In part, perhaps, because there is no sin or guilt yet. But shame also involves being unmasked; what is private and secret becomes public. Evidently the man and woman had no need to keep anything secret. There was only innocence and an utter lack of self-consciousness. Those point us on to the completion of this story.

Does the fact that the woman is created later and out of man make her an inferior creation? A later refinement? Neither? What of Paul's teaching that "the head of the woman is man" and "woman is the glory of man" (1 Cor. 11:3, 7-9)?

Do you think of our future blessed state as a return to what humans were in the Garden of Eden or as something even better? If better, in what ways?

CHAPTER 4

THE FALL
Genesis 3

Genesis 3 begins, rather abruptly, with the serpent. Who is this very crafty animal, and what role does it play in the story that follows?

The traditional view has been that Satan is speaking through this animal, although some have seen it as a mythological creature or a symbol of human curiosity. Notice that the text only says the serpent was one of "the wild animals the Lord God had made." That's all. No mention is made of Satan.

Notice also that much of this story is in direct discourse ("the serpent said . . . ," "the woman said . . . ," "the man said . . . ," "God said . . ."). That's typical of biblical narrative. It makes the people involved come alive in all their ambiguities of motive, purpose, and feelings.

Satan is later called "the tempter" (Matt. 4:3). Do you think Satan was speaking through the serpent? Is it right to insert into this text something taught later in the Bible? Explain.

A REAL SHAME

The serpent's first statement is manifestly false when compared with God's warning in 2:16-17. The woman corrects the serpent, adding the notion that even touching the fruit will cause death. Then the serpent flatly contradicts God (v. 4). They will not die, it says. Eating will open their eyes (a sort of magic) and make them like God. The serpent infers

What of this "you must not touch it"? Is Eve romanticizing God's command or making the tree a taboo? Is it wrong to add to God's command? Why?

that God is purposely, jealously, keeping the man and woman subordinate.

> **What is the appeal of this temptation? Does it appeal to the human senses? To a natural desire to know more? To human pride and ego?**

The next scene opens with the woman and the man standing before the forbidden tree. Sin often begins with us thinking about doing the wrong thing, considering the pluses and minuses. That's what seems to be happening here. But the woman sees only the pluses, so she takes the fruit and eats it. Her husband, evidently following her lead without question, accepts the fruit from her and eats also.

What the serpent promised happens. The man and woman are changed by eating the forbidden fruit. Their eyes are opened, but what they see is evidently not pleasant—they see their own nakedness and shame. Their original innocence is lost, and they feel exposed. So they try unsuccessfully to cover themselves, hiding their shame with sewn fig leaves.

CRIME AND PUNISHMENT

The third scene in this story is the "trial"—God convicts the serpent, the man, and the woman, and hands out their penalties (vv. 8-19). The scene opens with the telling picture of the man and the woman hiding from God like naughty children. But when God, in an act of grace, calls them, they appear. The man explains that their nakedness has not only caused shame but also fear of God.

> **Why did God ask this series of questions? To discover the answers? As a legal procedure? To make the man and woman aware of what they had done?**

Notice that we're not dealing here with two repentant sinners who voluntarily confess and seek forgiveness. God must pry the truth out of them, and even then they give it most reluctantly. Their pitiful defenses (vv. 12 and 13) admit their guilt while trying to shift the blame to someone or something else. So God announces their punishments.

Remember that the promised result of eating from the tree was that they would "surely die" (2:17). That's not mentioned in chapter 3 except indirectly (v. 19). In fact, Adam lives on for 930 years, although eventually he does die (5:5). So it seems that God graciously postpones death. The other major result of their sin is banishment from the garden (v. 23).

The three punishments mentioned here in poetic form (vv. 14-19) seem to be explanations of why things are so wrong in our present world. Why is there enmity between serpents and humans? Why is childbearing so painful? Why is a woman subordinate to her husband? Why is working the ground so difficult? The text reveals that these are all due to human sin.

Notice that only the serpent is directly cursed. The man and the woman are punished but not cursed, although the ground is cursed because of them. In the Bible a direct curse by God is only found here and in the case of Cain (4:11). God also ordains enmity between the serpent and the woman and their offspring. In other words, the Lord will not permit this unnatural alliance to continue.

The woman is evidently punished by increased pain in childbirth and by being subject to her husband. That's a change from the partnership they enjoyed before. The man is condemned to earning bread by hard toil instead of by the easier picking of the garden's fruit. He is tied to the earth and must labor there until death releases him.

Adam names his wife "Eve" (literally, *living*) because she will be the mother of all the living. And God graciously provides them with decent clothing made from skin. You get a sense here of the beginnings of civilization, of childbirth, and of wearing clothing—of the sort of life that the original readers of this text experienced.

Notice the reason given for the banishment from the garden. The man may not eat of the tree that will give everlasting life. That would negate the consequence of sin, which is death. An additional reason is given: outside the Garden of Eden the man must begin to till the ground. So the man and his wife are driven from the garden, and the way back is barred forever. This is a dark ending to a story that began so brightly.

Verse 15 is often called the "first gospel" and is seen as a promise of the struggle between Jesus Christ and Satan (Rom. 16:20). Is that reading too much into this verse? Or is it a legitimate interpretation?

This entire event has been described by some as a "fall upward." They see it as the beginning of human knowledge and civilization. Is that how the author understood it? How do you view it?

CHAPTER 5

CAIN AND ABEL
Genesis 4:1-17

The best-known Bible stories are often the most difficult to read carefully. The moralistic versions we learn in church school, hear in sermons, or even see in cartoons tend to block any true listening to the text. But when we take a closer look at the Cain and Abel story, we realize it is not primarily about the first murder but rather about Cain's relationship with God. Only secondarily is the story about Abel's relationship with his brother.

Genesis is full of rivalry between brothers—Cain and Abel, Ishmael and Isaac, Esau and Jacob, the ten older brothers and Joseph. In each case, God favors (elects) the younger, who is usually the weaker one and the most powerless. That same divine preference is noted and explained in Paul's letter, where he writes, "God chose the foolish . . . the weak . . . the despised things. . . " (1 Cor. 1:27-28). In addition to exploring Cain's relationship with God, this story is about God's mysterious choices.

> Why does Genesis speak so often about brothers? Why did Jesus (see Luke 15:11-32)? Why not sisters? Why not parent and child? In biblical times why might brothers be the most difficult family relationship?

CHOICES

The text begins by picturing a stable family. Eve has a son and triumphantly proclaims that she has "created" a man "with the help of the Lord" (v. 1). She names him Cain, which means "vitality." The second son gets no such attention; he is named Abel, which means "vapor" or "emptiness." Each son, we are told, brings an offering of the results of his labor to the Lord. Now comes the surprise. The Lord favors Abel's offering but not Cain's. Why this is so and how the brothers know it is so is not explained.

The temptation for the modern reader is to insert some explanation. We want a clear reason for God's favor or disfavor. A free God who acts independently from us and who seems to make arbitrary choices is an offense to us. We think God must have a reason for accepting Abel's sacrifice and rejecting Cain's. But this text gives no reason at all. Not even Hebrews 11:4, which speaks of Abel's "more acceptable sacrifice" offered by faith, fully explains the divine favor toward Abel's sacrifice and the rejection of Cain's.

> How do we react to such a temptation to sin? Do we say "I can't help it," or "It's in my genes," or "It's my parents' fault"? Or do we try to master it?

Cain's reaction to God's unexpected rejection is anger and sullenness. Notice that the text does not seem to condemn this emotional reaction. But the Lord does urge him to consider the "why" of his feelings. The Lord also warns him to "do well" and promises a divine blessing if he does so. Evidently sin has not yet entered Cain but is "crouching at the door" like a tiger. This seems to be a very graphic but powerful description of temptation. But note also that Cain must—and therefore, obviously, can—master it.

THE FIRST MURDER

Having once challenged Cain by rejecting his offering, the Lord now challenges him again—this time to resist temptation and to do the right thing. You see how this story focuses on the relationship between God and Cain as it continues to develop.

> C. S. Lewis described anger as the power to fight evil. Do you find this to be true? Or is that description too self-justifying and too much a temptation to sin? What did Jesus mean when he said that anger itself will lead to judgment (Matt. 5:21-26)?

Cain fails the test. The story of the actual murder is abrupt and stark. It takes only one verse made up of two sentences to convey Cain's dark deed. We're not told why Cain's anger against God was transferred to his envy of Abel. Nor are we provided with any excuse, such as "in a fit of rage Cain attacked Abel and. . . ." Obviously sin mastered Cain. This is how the first murder occurs.

Again God speaks to Cain (v. 9), giving him an opportunity to confess his sin. But Cain is no repentant sinner. When God asks, "Where is your brother Abel?" Cain's flat "I don't know" is a lie. His added infamous question, "Am I my brother's keeper?" is more than a mere ducking of the truth. It rejects any responsibility for another person's welfare, even if that other person is his own brother. Notice there is no trace here of any sense of guilt, even before the face of God.

God asks a last rhetorical question (v. 10), like the one he earlier asked of Eve (3:13). Then God makes the dramatic statement that Abel's blood is crying out from the ground. The lawsuit's investigation is ended. Cain's guilt is undeniable. So the Lord pronounces judgment.

In what ways does this story parallel the fall account? In what ways is it different?

THE SENTENCE

Notice that Cain is not killed—instead he is cursed. The ground that he tilled, the ground that swallowed Abel's blood, will no longer yield him crops. His way of living is taken away. Cain is also banished from the community of human beings. This man who disclaimed any responsibility for his brother's welfare will now lose the welfare and protection that the clan has provided. Truly the punishment fits the crime.

Cain's lament about the severity of this punishment focuses on the danger he will experience as a fugitive and wanderer. Away from the clan anyone can kill him. This reflects the situation at the time this text was written. Protection from others did not come from police or from an army, but from the clan. So a fugitive was highly vulnerable. God responds by putting a mark on Cain to prevent this initial murder from leading to more killings. So Cain goes away "from the presence of the Lord" to the land of Nod, which means *misery* or *restlessness*. There he continues to live.

Are the rabbis right in thinking that the mark was circumcision? Or was the mark a tattoo? Or an unusual hairstyle? Why is this mark not explained?

This story tells of a challenge from God, a temptation to sin, a murder, divine judgment on it, and unexpected mercy even though Cain never seems to repent of his sin. It is a terrible and wonderful story that teaches us about God's dealings with the first humans. It has much to teach us also about God's dealings with us.

Does God challenge each of us in seemingly unfair and arbitrary ways? How do we respond? Do you consider this a case of "the Lord disciplines those he loves" (Heb. 12:6)? Why or why not?

Chapter 6

The Flood
Genesis 6:5-7:24

Another very familiar story is that of Noah and the great flood. Because it's such a lengthy one, we'll divide it into two parts. As you read this story, notice the number of detailed descriptions and striking repetitions. This is typical of certain narrative sections of the Bible. They stand in sharp contrast to our modern writing style. Each time you encounter this, ask yourself why the detail or repetition is being included. You will probably find that the answers will vary from one case to the next.

Three actions of the Lord bind the first three verses together: the Lord "saw," "was grieved," and "said" (vv. 5-7). The Lord concluded that the earth was in a very sorry state. Not only the deeds, but even the plans and thoughts of human beings, were intolerably wicked. Notice the extremely emphatic words "every," "only," and "all the time" (v. 5). Notice also the pervasive tone of deep sadness in these verses.

Consider some of the possible reasons for so much repetition. Could it be because the story was originally an oral one? Or was it due to a more leisurely life rhythm in those times? Or were two different accounts combined? Could repetition help to emphasize certain points of the story? If so, which ones?

Storm Clouds Gather

Contrary to our usual notion of God as a lofty judge untouched by human acts, this text speaks of deep divine sorrow and grief over humanity's wickedness. One might compare

> Why didn't God give a warning? Why did the Lord not send a prophet like Jonah? Is it because a warning always includes the possibility of forgiveness?

> Why was Noah's family included in this salvation? Was it because they were only an extension of him? Or were they needed for the future? Or were they included because the Bible thinks in terms of family units?

God here to a master potter or painter whose work of art does not meet his standards of excellence. It must therefore be destroyed, regardless of how painful that act may be. So the Lord resolves to destroy the earth, especially this creature made to be God's own representative and governor over all other creatures. Notice that all the animals are included—as if that were inevitable—in this anticipated destruction of humankind.

But—and there is a tremendous surprise and wonder in this "but"—one man finds favor in the Lord's sight. Notice how the decision to save Noah follows immediately on the decision to destroy humankind. Notice also that the text does not give the reason for saving Noah. Evidently it does not lie in this man's righteousness. That characteristic is not mentioned until the following verse. Verse 8 tells us flatly that God has made a mysterious and wonderful decision to save this single human being.

Verses 11-13 provide the first extensive repetition. They repeat in other words what has already been told in earlier verses. This time, however, the emphasis falls on the earth's pervasive violence and utter corruption, in contrast to the goodness of the original creation mentioned in 1:31. Also, God now speaks directly to Noah, telling him of the imminent destruction.

Notice the extent of this destruction—"all life"—expressed most clearly in verse 17.

THE ARK

The instructions for building the ark are very detailed. Like a divine blueprint, they lay out the precise materials and dimensions. In this ark God proposes to save not only Noah and his entire family but also at least two representatives of every living creature. Though all the other animals will perish along with the corrupt people, at least two of every species will be preserved with this favored family.

> How long do you think it took Noah and his sons to build this gigantic ark? Why was this task left to them while the animals were evidently gathered by God (7:15)? In what ways might faith in the word of God be more difficult when it involves much work over a long period of time?

The chapter concludes with a verse which, if you were reading this text aloud, would receive great weight and emphasis: "Noah . . . did everything just as God commanded him" (6:22). All these detailed, elaborate instructions Noah followed precisely. The passage highly commends him for his obedience.

Notice that nothing is said about the reactions of neighbors or fellow townspeople to the ark-building project. Biblical narrative is very economical, often ignoring matters that we consider highly interesting.

Again the Lord speaks to Noah. How the Lord does this—in a vision, a dream, or a voice from heaven—the text does not say. Again God gives Noah precise instructions and details about what will happen and when the flood will occur (in seven days). Again special note is made of the fact that Noah does everything the Lord commands (7:5).

Verses 6-16 of chapter 7 give us a virtual repetition of what God said would happen, adding details such as Noah's age (600), the precise day the flood began (February 17 by our calendar), and the fact that the animals all "came to Noah and entered the ark" (v. 15). Try to picture this awesome procession as the animals enter the ark in a miraculously orderly way. Notice that after they've all gone in, it isn't Noah, but the Lord, who shuts up the ark.

THE FLOOD

Interspersed through this account is a description of the flood itself (vv. 11-12). Like a waterlogged balloon that bursts, the "springs of the great deep" gush out over the land. Without the usual clouds, the waters flow down out of the heavens as if its windows (floodgates) have been allowed to fly open. The imagery is one of an irresistible, overflowing flood that drowns the earth.

The last paragraphs (vv. 17-24) further describe the flood. Notice how they refer again and again to "the waters" as they swell ever deeper and higher. Remember that to the people of Palestine, with its semi-arid climate, unrestrained waters represented chaos and death.

So the first part of this story ends with Noah and his family and all the animals safely in the ark as it rides the waters of the flood. They are safe. But they are alone, traumatized, and fearful of what the future may hold. Only their faith in God sustains them.

> Since some people cannot imagine that the water could have covered the world's highest mountain ranges, they think the flood was limited to the Mesopotamian area. Do you agree? If true, would that nullify this story? Or would it still remain a proclamation of God's severe judgment and great mercy? Why?

> Notice the great seriousness of God in dealing with human wickedness. Does it remind you more of an angry tyrant, a frustrated perfectionist, a disappointed lover, or a grieving parent?

Chapter 7

Rainbows
Genesis 8:1-9:17

The second part of the flood story opens with a statement reminiscent of the report in 6:8 that Noah had "found favor" with the Lord. This time we are told that God "remembered" Noah and all the animals. This does not mean that God had conveniently forgotten about these survivors for the last 150 days. When the term *remember* is used in the Bible, it usually implies God's merciful and saving action (see the description of God's response to Rachel's prayer in Genesis 30:22).

For those in the ark, salvation begins with a gradual receding of the waters. God has closed the springs and floodgates and now sends a drying wind. The waters begin to subside.

> Just as the waters of the flood are said to prefigure baptism (1 Pet. 3:20-21), the ark is often taken as a symbol of the church. What similarities do you find between the two? What differences? Do you like this analogy?

A Long Wait

Notice the precise dates given for when the ark comes to rest on the mountaintop and for when land became visible. Including these dates makes clear the length of the flood. It started in the second month, but not until the beginning of the tenth month do the tops of the mountains appear. Do you sense the anxious waiting of this family as the weeks and months stretch out without any inkling of when the flood will recede and life might return to normal?

> Imagine the conditions in the ark. How were all the animals fed? Watered? Cleaned? What would a typical day have been like for Noah and his family?

Why has the dove bearing an olive leaf become a modern symbol of peace?

Now follow the stories about the birds that Noah sent out to test how far the waters had receded (8:6-12). Note how each sending reflects a growing impatience. Noah's action may anticipate an ancient custom of keeping birds on a ship and releasing them to determine the direction to land. It also shows animals serving humans in a trust relationship.

Finally, on Noah's six-hundredth birthday, Noah removes the covering from the ark (8:13). Three hundred seventy-five days after the rains began, the earth is finally dry (7:11 and 8:14). Now comes the command to go out of the ark. Again Noah obeys. Notice the implied blessing of fertility that the Lord gives to the animals that have survived the flood (8:17).

Noah gives the appropriate response to being saved—a thank offering to God. He seems to sacrifice an inordinately large number of animals (8:20). The presumption appears to be that, since the animals have propagated during the year on the ark, there were enough of them for some to be available for sacrifice without endangering the species.

GOD'S BLESSING

Does the image of the Lord being pleased with Noah's sacrifices and resolving to continue the days and seasons fit with your idea of God? Or does this divine reversal seem too quick and radical?

There follows a remarkable statement: God was "pleased" with the odor of this sacrifice and made a decision never again to curse the ground or to destroy every living creature. This is a major divine reversal. From now on, in spite of humanity's continuing wickedness, "[God] causes his sun to rise on the evil and the good, and sends rain on the righteous and the unrighteous" (Matt. 5:45). In other words, God will not let human rebellion thwart his grand purposes for creation. This resolve makes possible a new beginning based on the abiding rhythms of life sustained by its Creator.

Note that the phrase "said in his heart" (8:21) does not indicate some deeper level of decision. Biblical narratives are characterized by much direct discourse. This phrase indicates direct discourse with oneself. In other words, it means "said to him- or herself" or, simply, "thought."

The story of the flood concludes with two additional sections. The first tells how God blesses and sanctifies all of life. The second details the divine promise never again to destroy all living creatures by a flood. Note how these sections are carefully organized, with the opening sentences (9:1 and 9:8) almost repeated in the closing sentences (9:7 and 9:17).

The first section reasserts the dominance of humans over all other creatures, but with a new tone. Now human rule is accompanied by fear and dread. Now all other creatures must serve humans, even to the point of providing them with food. There is a new tension in creation that contrasts the peace and harmony of the beginning.

Notice the added restriction not to eat meat with its lifeblood in it. Blood was the symbol of pulsing life in the Bible (see Deut. 12:23). Life must be gone before flesh may be used as meat. This restriction prevents bloodthirstiness and brutality.

Human blood, however, may never be shed at all. Notice the thrice repeated "I will demand an accounting. . . ." As image-bearers, humans hold a higher status. God requires that human life be treated with respect and reverence.

A SINGLE-SIDED COVENANT

The last section details the covenant God establishes with Noah, with all the human race, and with all creatures. Notice the lack of the usual covenantal "if" clause requiring human faith or obedience (compare Gen. 12:1-2; 17:1-2; Ex. 19:5-6).

This covenant is all from one side as God unilaterally promises never again to destroy the earth.

The sign of the covenant—the rainbow—and what it will mean to God ("I will remember my covenant") is mentioned four times (9:13, 14-15, 16, 17). This repetition, like a clock tolling, signals the gravity of God's promise and the beginning of a new stage in human life. Notice that the rainbow is meant to remind *God*, not us, of this covenant. Notice also the many phrases that emphasize the continuing validity and universality of this covenant.

The flood is remarkable for the author of this text but not because of its destructive force. It is remarkable because of the change it brings in divine policy. God promises to bear with human beings, to work to bring them back into a loving relationship, and to craft a way of salvation for all who will turn to their Lord in faith and obedience.

In Genesis 1:29 God gave humans all the seeds and fruits for food. Now flesh is added (9:3). Do you think everyone before Noah was vegetarian? Or did they eat meat without divine approval?

The modern "sanctity of life" notion includes all living creatures. This text seems to sanctify only human life. Which idea do you think is right? Why?

The flood story tells us how God changed his mind about how to treat creation. Do you find this idea strange? A mere anthropomorphism? Inappropriate to your concept of God? A reassuring notion of divine grace? Why?

CHAPTER 8

BABEL
Genesis 11:1-9

This compact little story should trigger the question "Why is this account included in the Bible?" That's a good question to ask about every Bible story, of course, because it makes us think about the purpose and meaning of each account. It's particularly appropriate to ask about this story because, on initial reading, its purpose seems rather obscure. Remember that the Bible does not include any story just because it might be of historical interest. It is not an academic history book but an account of God's way of salvation. Every narrative included contributes in some way to our understanding of that salvation and of the God who graciously offers it.

This story is about language. Most human traditions assume that the multiplicity of languages is somehow unnatural, and each tradition offers some sort of explanation of this phenomenon. Probably that's the common reaction of isolated peoples who have always known only one language and are then suddenly confronted with a strange tongue. This story asserts that in the beginning only one language was spoken by all people. This is prior to the diversity of languages referred to in the preceding chapter (10:5, 20, 31).

> **Why do you think this story is included in the Bible? To explain the multiplicity of languages? To describe the scattering of the people? To show a divine thwarting of human pride? To set the stage for the calling of Abram?**

> **How does the deep biblical interest in language and "the word" fit with our present emphasis on images and pictures (consider TV and advertising)?**

STICKING TOGETHER

> Who are the "they" of these verses? All the people on earth? All the children of Noah? Or one particular group of people?

In 11:2 we are told that "they" (the people) had migrated to a valley in Mesopotamia—probably the plain where the city of Babylon was later located. Finding water, food, and peace, they settled there. Nothing is said to indicate any transition from a nomadic to a sedentary life.

Beginning with verse 3, notice the repeated "us" and "we" terminology that seems to indicate a tight, cohesive community. In other words, this is an organized people, able to plan and work well together. They resolve, we are told in verse 4, to build a city and a tower. Lacking the stone and mortar used in Palestine for building, they spend a year making bricks and preparing the needed tar—the standard building materials in the Mesopotamian region—in order to accomplish their goal. Then they begin to build.

Notice how the text carefully details their reasons for building the tower and the city: to "make a name for [them]selves" and to prevent themselves from being scattered abroad. The text makes no judgment about these reasons. Nothing is said to indicate that they are bad.

> Is it wrong to seek to be a unified community with a name? Isn't a church such a group? How does self-seeking unity differ from unity in Christ?

However, in light of the fact that God puts a decided stop to their efforts, it is safe to assume that the people are somewhat misguided. Evidently they seek a self-serving unity in contrast to a covenantal unity with God. Their desire for "a name" may reflect an ambition similar to Adam and Eve's: to be like God (3:5). And their resistance to being scattered might be at odds with the divine mandate to "fill the earth and subdue it" (1:28). Finally, the design of the tower "that reaches to the heavens" (11:4) seems to indicate a sinful pride—although this may also reflect how early Jews, unused to tall buildings, viewed the towers of Babylon. Those ziggurats, as the towers were called, had names expressing that same ambition, such as "The House of the Link between Heaven and Earth."

BABBLE AT BABEL

> What limits did God impose on human beings from the beginning? Why do we need limits? What limits do we try to exceed? Have we exceeded God's limits with the creation of nuclear weaponry? With cloning?

Beginning with verse 5, we see the Lord's reaction to this people's plans and ambitions. Note the anthropomorphic language used in picturing God as coming down to view their work in progress. The united power and ambition of these people appears to have been a red flag to the Lord. In the Bible's view, God is the only one with whom nothing is impossible (see Gen. 18:14; Job 42:2). No one may say, "I will make myself like the Most High" (Isa. 14:14). Humans must always recognize their limits.

A common language is vital to forming and maintaining a community. It permits communication and it shapes and defines the fellowship. So God destroys this community by confusing their language. They are no longer able to hear and understand each other.

> **Have you ever experienced confusion of language? What were the results? Did it lead to scattering?**

This event is often contrasted with the Pentecost occurrence where the Holy Spirit gave the disciples the ability "to speak in other languages" (Acts 2:4). The Spirit's gifts at Pentecost laid the foundation for a new community based not only on sharing a common faith but also in having all things in common (Acts 2:44). This new community was able to spread the gospel throughout the Roman empire.

Without a common language the building project proved impossible. As they feared, the people were "scattered . . . abroad over the face of the earth" (v. 9). So this frustrated project came to be called *Babel*, meaning *confused*. As so often in Scripture, the divine act gave the final name to this location, identifying its role in divine history.

So ends the Bible's general human history. The stage has been set for what will be the primary story of how God chose one couple, one people, one nation, and, finally, how God sent his only Son to bring about reconciliation between God and straying, sinful human beings. Everything up to now has been necessary background for the real story of salvation which begins with Abram.

> **Do you see the divine intervention at Babel as a punishment for prideful ambition? Or is it an act of grace by which God prevented a human disaster? Explain.**

CHAPTER 9

GOD'S CALL TO ABRAM
Genesis 11:27-12:9

This story signals a shift in the book of Genesis and in the biblical narrative until the book of Acts. The divine focus narrows from the entire human race and its representatives to one person, one family, and, eventually, one nation. Not that "all the peoples on earth" are forgotten! But any blessing to them will come only through the line of Abram—as eventually salvation for all who believe will come only through Jesus Christ.

The story begins with the family of Terah who lives in Ur of the Chaldees in southern Mesopotamia. The family includes Terah's son Abram (which means "exalted father") and his wife Sarai ("princess"), another son Nahor and his wife Milcah ("queen"), and a grandson Lot, whose father Haran has died. Sarai is Abram's half sister (20:12), and Milcah is Nahor's niece. Custom evidently approved such marriages.

Sarai is barren. Note that the announcement is repeated for emphasis. This introduces what becomes a major theme in the Bible. Think of Rebekah, Rachel, Samson's mother, Hannah, and Elizabeth. Barrenness is a biblical symbol of human emptiness, futility, frustration, and lack of hope for the future. Only God has the power to change that, giving "life to the dead" (Rom. 4:17).

> Why do you think God chose to work in this narrowed way? Is it fair to all those millions of other people?

> What do you think of these interfamily marriages? Why do you suppose that practice permitted in the past is forbidden now?

> What signs can you see in our culture that many people have lost the belief that God is the only source of life?

Terah and his family leave Ur, heading for Canaan. We're not told why they left or why they stopped at Haran. Evidently those reasons aren't important to the biblical author, so they're not included.

GOD CALLS

Now, suddenly, without any preamble or explanation, the Word of the Lord comes to Abram. After ten generations of silence, God speaks. Notice that there is no attempt to explain how God spoke, whether by vision, by dream, or directly. We also don't learn how Abram knew the speaker was God. The Word of God just comes! Just as that Word brought forth a new world at creation, now it brings forth a new people and a new future.

The pilgrim journey is a biblical metaphor for the life of faith. Why? In what ways does it speak also to *your* faith life?

God's Word comes as a command and a promise. First comes the command to leave land, kinsmen, and nuclear family. The triple leaving emphasizes the completeness of Abram's turning his back on everything familiar and venturing out into an unknown future. Notice that his destination is not given. Abram must set out in faith "to the land I will show you" (12:1).

Next comes the promise given in the form of a brief poem. Notice the seven elements of the promise:

Think of the times when you have been richly blessed (baptism, marriage, close of worship . . .) What did the blessing mean to you? How did it change your life?

> I will make you into a great nation
> and I will bless you;
> I will make your name great,
> and you will be a blessing.
> I will bless those who bless you,
> and whoever curses you I will curse;
> and all the peoples on earth
> will be blessed through you (Genesis 12:2).

ABRAM FOLLOWS

Promises seem to be God's way of creating a new people and a new future. Unlike the creation of the world by the divine Word, this creative promise leaves room for a human response. The promise is a challenge as well as a hope. It appeals to normal human desire—the idea of becoming a great nation and becoming famous spoke to Abram's heart. But to attain those things requires Abram to take a radical step in faith and trust. The promise proves to be tremendously disruptive because it demands that Abram leave his family. And the promise will continue to cause future disruption as well by provoking struggles between parents, brothers, and sisters. Still, the promise becomes the center of the patriarchs' lives.

In response to the divine command, Abram leaves. Silent, unwavering obedience to the divine will is characteristic of this patriarch. God says "Go," and Abram goes. The author of this text includes no details that would diminish this pattern of call and instant response. Such economy of words is typical of the Bible. Any additional details such as that Lot goes along, that the family prospered at Haran, or Abram's age are always given for a reason that usually becomes clear later in the book. Always note which details are included and which are not.

Think of the family discussions and debates that must have raged when Abram announced he was going! Where? Don't know. Why? God told me to. How would you have reacted if you were in Abram's family?

Notice that there is not a word about the long, difficult journey; we're just told that they arrive in Canaan. Once there they trek through the land in a typically nomadic style. In this sparsely settled country, the Canaanites are the real residents. Abram and his clan are only nomads. They stop, pitch their tents, stay for a while. But when the grass is gone, when some difficulty arises with the local people, or when they get restless, they pack up everything and move on to a new location. Note the contrast to their life in Haran where they had settled down. God's call brought about a complete change of lifestyle as well as of location.

Staking a Claim

At Shechem the Lord again speaks to Abram, this time appearing before him. That greater intimacy is matched with a greater specificity in the promise. Now Abram is told that this land where he stands is the promised future home of his descendants. This brief word of God binds the people of Israel to this promised land from that time on.

Do you think Palestine is still the promised land for all Jews? Or did that promise become void with Christ?

In Shechem and again in Ai, Abram builds an altar and presumably offers sacrifices. We are told that at Ai he "called on the name of the Lord" (v. 8). In gratitude for the Lord's appearance and promise, Abram now makes it his custom to build an altar and to worship wherever he stops.

If God told you to leave all your loved ones behind and go and live in a foreign land, how would you respond? What promise would make you willing to take such a radical step? Is conversion just such a command and promise? Explain.

In a sense the altar lays claim to the land. It becomes a marker and a memorial, a sign that this is a sacred place. There is no priest or cult, just Abram leading his family and all his clan in the worship of the living God who appears to him and talks with him.

CHAPTER 10

HAGAR AND ISHMAEL
Genesis 16

It has been ten years since Abram and Sarai arrived in Canaan. During this decade they have been living with the promise that they will birth a great nation. Yet Sarai remains barren. Abram has asked God about this matter and has been told, "A son coming from your own body will be your heir" (15:4). Nothing has been said, however, about this being Sarai's child as well. That comes later in Genesis 17:16.

As you read this story, note the new insights it gives us into the personalities of Abram and Sarai and of their marriage relationship. The story also traces the origins of the Ishmaelites, a roving desert people who were kin to the Israelites. Some of them later buy Joseph and sell him into Egyptian slavery (37:27).

TRYING TO FIND THEIR WAY

As the story opens, Sarai has become increasingly frustrated with her childless state. She does not deny the divine promise, but she decides to take action by designing a way to provide a son for Abram and a family for herself—notice the strong "I" statements in verses 2 and 5. She follows the accepted custom of arranging for a concubine to carry out the function of childbirth.

Notice how God's promises gradually grow more specific. This continues up to Jesus' birth. Why is this? To test our faith? To strengthen it? Or because we can't accept or make sense of it all right away?

Do you think it was wrong or unbelieving of Sarai and Abram to take this action? Does faith require that we wait passively for God to act? Don't we pray for healing but at the same time take medicine? Or is that different? How do we know when we should be passive and when we should act?

45

Hagar is referred to as Sarai's Egyptian maidservant. She is probably a slave girl, given to Sarai by her parents at the time of her marriage. Hagar serves as Sarai's personal maid and is responsible solely to her. Remember that later both Rachel and Leah have personal maids who become concubines of Jacob (30:3, 9). Notice how Sarai ponders, "Perhaps I can build a family through her" (v. 2). Evidently Hagar's child would be adopted by Sarai. The text doesn't make clear whether at this point Sarai completely despairs of having a child of her own. It may be that she shares the widespread belief that a woman may sometimes be able to become pregnant after adopting a child.

> **How do you explain to a child or to a new Christian this practice of polygamy as we find it recorded in Scripture?**

Abram doesn't object to his wife's scheme, and he does what Sarai tells him to do. The text makes no moral judgment about this couple's actions. Nor does it condemn this attempt to provide an heir as if it constituted a lack of faith on their part. In fact, God blesses the relationship and Hagar conceives.

CONFLICT

But now events take a new turn, one that should not have been entirely unexpected. Hagar, the slave girl, who up until now has been submissive to her mistress, begins to consider herself the better of the two. She now treats Sarai with contempt. We're not told what she says or does but it is probably some public act that is intensely humiliating for Sarai. In the book of Genesis, men argue about living space and food supply, but women fight over their position in the community.

> **Is this still true today? Are women more socially conscious than men or is that only a tired stereotype?**

Why does Sarai turn on Abram and blame him? The phrase "May the Lord judge between you and me" expresses anger, resentment, and a deep sense of having been wronged. But why does she herself not deal with Hagar? After all, Sarai is Abram's wife and the mistress of the household. But Sarai makes this an issue of justice between herself and her husband. It seems that in those days a slave was responsible to one person only. Hagar had belonged to Sarai but had been given to Abram as a concubine. So she had passed from Sarai's control to Abram's. Since Abram has done nothing to stop Hagar's abuse, Sarai must now appeal to her husband for justice.

> **With whom do your sympathies lie? With Sarai? Hagar? Abram? Would you judge Abram's action to be smart or cowardly? Do you think Sarai's abuse of Hagar is justified?**

Abram, we're told, turns Hagar over to Sarai. Sarai proceeds to abuse her, probably reducing her status from concubine back to slave and punishing her physically. The situation becomes so bad that the slave girl flees into the desert, preferring possible death to the misery of her life with Sarai.

God Hears

In the desert, by a spring, a man comes up to Hagar and begins talking to her. This is an angel, but Hagar speaks to him as though he were just an ordinary person. Only after she hears his prophetic words does she seem to realize that God has been speaking to her through him.

Still, there is something decidedly odd about this messenger. Hagar must have noticed. He knows her by name and knows her status: "servant of Sarai" (v. 8). And with unmistakable authority he instructs her to go back to her mistress and submit to her. Then comes an annunciation, a message of blessing and promise like that addressed to Mary and Elizabeth. Sarai wanted to build a family by using this slave girl. Now God promises to build *Hagar* into a people "too numerous to count" (v. 10).

She will have a son who will be named Ishmael, which means "God hears." The description that follows evidently fits the Jewish ideas about the nature of the Ishmaelite people. They will be a sturdy folk, like the untamable wild donkey. They will be fearless and fleet of foot—a separate, warlike people who are tightly tribal. In other words, they will be a bedouin people.

Hagar recognizes that God has both seen her and spoken to her. Her statement identifies the messenger with the Lord himself. We find the same thing in the story of Abraham at Mamre, where the three men who visit Abraham first appear as plain human visitors. But later in the story one of them is identified as the Lord (18:2, 10).

The story assumes that Hagar does as the angel directs, returning to Sarai and submitting to her. The baby is born. Abram is the one who names the child Ishmael—an indication that he recognizes him as his own son and makes him an heir. For a conclusion to the story of Hagar and Ishmael we must jump forward to Genesis 21:8-21. For now, however, the narrative picks up the thread of a child of greater promise, that of Isaac, son of Abram and son of Sarai.

Why does God intervene? Because Hagar carries Abram's child? Because of divine sympathy for the abused and enslaved?

What does this story teach us about God's ways? Doesn't the Lord seem to allow Abram, Sarai, and Hagar a lot of latitude? Why are God's interventions so limited yet so dramatic?

Chapter 11

Meeting at Mamre
Genesis 18:1-15

Genesis 17:5 told us how God dramatically sealed the promise to Abram by changing his name to *Abraham*, which means "father of many." Now the narrative announces the momentous occasion when "The Lord appeared to Abraham" (18:1). But what it portrays is a very ordinary domestic scene. The clan is camped under the trees at Mamre. It's the middle of the day, and everyone is dozing. Abraham looks up and sees three men who have approached undetected and who are politely standing nearby, waiting to be greeted.

Why does the story begin by referring to Abraham's guests as "three men" and only later identify one of them as "the Lord"?

Hosting God

Notice what happens next. The narrative supplies a quick succession of action verbs, all applying to Abraham. He sees, he hurries, he bows low, he speaks, he hurries again, he runs to get a calf, he brings food to the men, and he stands courteously and waits while they eat. The first eight verses are full of Abraham's almost frantic efforts—remarkable, we would think, in a man ninety-nine years old. All this for strangers who are clearly not invited to stay over! Note Abraham's closing remark "and then go on your way" (18:5). Why all this frantic activity?

Notice also the exceedingly polite language Abraham uses in verses 3-5. It's almost as if he is addressing royalty. The

The ambiguity of whether the English "you" is plural or singular does not occur in Scripture. For example, in John 16:13 the two pronouns "you" in that passage are clearly in the plural. Does that make an important difference in how we should understand that text?

What moral tenet is most central to your own ethic? Not stealing? No abortions? Sunday observance? What moral rule do you drum into your children? Is hospitality important to you? Who do you practice it with? Family and friends? Church members? Strangers?

way that Abraham speaks to one of the men indicates that he is clearly the leader while the other two are his attendants. Because the English "you" does not distinguish between singular and plural as the Hebrew does, we lose sight of this fact—the verbs in verse 3 are singular, while those in verses 4 and 5 are plural. In any event, Abraham is extremely courteous despite the fact that these strangers are undoubtedly dusty and scruffy from their morning travel. He does not realize until later that one of them is actually the Lord (v. 10). So why this very polite treatment?

The answer lies in the vital importance of hospitality in Abraham's moral universe. This is far more than bedouin courtesy or the custom of the day. While Lot shows similar hospitality, the people of Sodom are eager to abuse the two visitors (19:1-8). Later on in biblical history, willingness to serve and welcome strangers becomes the standard by which Abraham's servant chooses a bride for Isaac (24:14, 17-20). Moses forbids any mistreatment or oppression of strangers (Ex. 22:21; 23:9; Lev. 19:33). Welcoming strangers is mentioned as one of the ways in which followers should serve Jesus (Matt. 25:35). And hospitality is a prime virtue in the early church (1 Tim. 5:10; Heb. 13:2). So Abraham's righteousness, displayed in this zealous hospitality, prepares the way—by contrast—to the story of the sin and destruction of Sodom that follows.

LAUGHTER

With verse nine the entire tone and tempo of the story changes. The strangers take control of the conversation. They know Sarah's name. One is called "the Lord." And the talk suddenly turns slow, deliberate, and weighty.

The strangers begin with a courteous question that turns attention to Sarah. This is followed by an announcement of the time when Sarah will have a son. The divine promise has unfolded in stages. First came the promise of producing a great nation (12:2), then the promise that the heir would be Abram's natural-born son (15:4). Next came the promise that this would be Sarah's child (17:16). And now a time is given for the long-awaited event.

There is nothing sneaky about Sarah listening from the tent. That was accepted practice in the days when wives were not permitted to appear before strangers.

Sarah hears and laughs. Abraham also had laughed when he had been told earlier that Sarah would bear him a son

(17:17). This laughter is obviously the key to the second part of this story, but how are we to interpret it? Is it a surprised, "So this is actually going to happen" laugh? Is it a joyful, "Me, I'm going to have a *baby*" laugh? Is it a skeptical, "Sure I'm going to have a baby, hah, hah" laugh? Or is it a scornful, "This guy doesn't seem to understand female biology" laugh?

Notice how the text leaves the question open-ended. It doesn't say Sarah laughed joyfully, or unbelievingly, or scornfully. It just says she "laughed to herself" (v. 12). The phrase "to herself" is important because the Lord responds by asking Abraham, "Why did she laugh and say to herself . . ." (v. 13). That statement, more than any other, identifies the speaker as someone who is more than human, who hears the unspoken, and who knows the thoughts of the heart.

How do you understand Abraham's and Sarah's laughter? What sort of news makes you laugh?

Then we come to one of those phrases—here in the form of a question—that surfaces unexpectedly in the Bible as a fundamental challenge to faith: "Is anything too hard for the Lord?" (v. 14). That question seems to imply that Sarah's laughter expressed a belief that even God couldn't enable her to bear a child at her advanced age. But again this is not explicitly stated. The question just stands there unanswered.

Why is this phrased as a question? Jesus made it a statement (Mark 10:27). What does the answer say about God's nature? About your faith in God?

THE QUESTION

Sarah is afraid because she realizes that this person is the Lord. So she lies. She tries to withdraw her laughter, to take away the offense, to smooth over what has become an embarrassing situation. You might call this a "social lie." But the divine messenger responds flatly and impolitely, "Yes, you did laugh" (v. 15).

There the story ends, with Sarah's laughter and the question "Is anything too hard for the Lord?" Both are left for this couple and for the reader to think about. What more powerful ending could there be to this story?

Do you think of faith as a venturing out in response to a divine call or as waiting for a divine promise to be fulfilled? What practical difference would this make?

Chapter 12

A Challenge to God's Justice
Genesis 18:16-33

In modern translations, the subheads given in chapters 18 and 19 tend to be misleading. The NRSV makes it "Judgment Pronounced on Sodom." But that only refers to the setting for the conversation between the Lord and Abraham. The NIV interprets it as "Abraham Pleads for Sodom," which tends to make Abraham into a mere humanitarian and confuses the point of the questions he is asking. So in your reading of this text, ignore whatever subheads your Bible version has given this story.

The three men—not *mere* men, as we have discovered—leave the camp and descend the heights toward Sodom. Out of courtesy Abraham walks along with them for a while. As they walk along, the Lord begins to confide in Abraham—as a friend. Recognize, however, that the model of this friendship in the Bible is not that of two equal chums but of a king who chooses someone to be his confidante, telling this person what is kept secret from everyone else (see Amos 3:7). So God's friendship here is tied to confiding certain hidden knowledge. Jesus calls his disciples "friends" in exactly this same sense (John 15:15).

The Lord mentions Abraham's unique status and promised future. God points also to the astonishing intimacy that exists between them. The word translated as "chosen"

In our culture friendship is the ideal relationship. Spouses want to be friends and parents want to be friends with their children. But doesn't friendship require equality? So how can we be Jesus' friends since Jesus is our Lord?

Why add the condition here? To qualify the praise? To emphasize the importance of doing justice? To show the importance of instructing children?

really means "known" and indicates the existence of a close bond. Abraham's task is to "keep the way of the Lord." This involves doing "what is right and just" and seeing to it that his children and household do the same (v. 19). Note that this is the condition on which the Lord gives all the promised blessings. This is the first clear conditional that we find in the Abraham stories.

Why this little speech by the Lord to Abraham? Why this prelude to talking about the possible destruction of Sodom and Gomorrah? The text does not say. But given what follows, it would seem this is intended to put Abraham enough at ease to be able to ask God some difficult questions.

A Fearsome Secret

What is the "sin" of Sodom? Homosexual practices? Oppression? Lack of hospitality? See Ezekiel 16:49-50.

Now the Lord tells Abraham of the great outcry that has been rising to heaven against the cities of the plain—as later the cries of the slaves in Egypt will be heard by God (Ex. 3:7). The Lord assumes the role of judge but does not rush to judgment. He first comes down to investigate how bad the sin really is. What a remarkable image!

But God knows, as Abraham also knows, that the people of the cities are truly evil. So the destruction of Sodom and Gomorrah is assumed to be a settled matter in the conversation that follows.

Why does God consult with Abraham over the plan to destroy Sodom? Because of Lot? For a second opinion? Out of courtesy? Out of regard for Abraham? Or to give Abraham a chance to ask some hard questions?

What is Abraham doing? Praying for divine mercy for Sodom? Haggling for Lot's life? Or inquiring about God's justice?

Now we come to the heart of the story. The two men/angels head down to Sodom to check out the extent of its sin. What happens there is told in the next chapter. But Abraham and the Lord remain standing together. Some older versions of the text say "God remained standing before Abraham," inviting his comments and criticism (v. 22). That reading was later changed by scribes who probably considered such an idea inappropriate.

Abraham asks the Lord a question (vv. 23-25). Pay close attention to what Abraham says to God in these verses. This has been interpreted as Abraham's finest moment (according to Bloom), as a human declaration of independence from God's absolute monarchy (says Fromm), and as a new notion of divine justice (says Brueggemann).

Be clear about what Abraham is *not* asking for. He is not asking God to rescue the righteous people out of the doomed cities. That is what actually happens, as the angels escort Lot and his family out of Sodom. He is not asking for divine mercy for these wicked people. Rather he is urging God to act justly—"Will not the judge of all the earth do right?" (v. 25).

Abraham may well have been moved to humanitarian pity at the thought of all these thousands of people being swept away. But that is not what he talks about to God.

Abraham never challenges God's right to destroy the wicked. But he does challenge the justice of also destroying the righteous, as if there is no difference between the righteous and the wicked. To sweep them away together, to treat them alike, would in Abraham's eyes constitute a gross injustice. The Old Testament is more concerned about how God treats the righteous than with the way God treats the wicked—think, for example, of Job and of Psalm 1.

FOR JESUS' SAKE

Abraham goes on to ask whether God won't also spare the wicked *for the sake of* the righteous. The lengthy reduction of the number of righteous required from fifty down to ten makes the question more pointed. It also seems to merge a concern for the extent of divine justice and a plea for divine mercy even on the wicked. Notice that the text leaves the tone of Abraham's request of God unresolved.

The text returns again and again to the phrase "for the sake of the righteous." This is the basis for Abraham's inquiry as to whether God will spare the city. Does that seem strange to you? Remember Jesus' parable about the wheat and the weeds (Matt. 13:24ff.). It is for the sake of the wheat that the weeds are spared, at least until harvesttime arrives.

Remember also that the forgiveness of our sins is for the sake of Christ's righteousness. The New Testament, in a sense, refines Abraham's question even further to ask whether God will spare the wicked for the sake of one righteous person. And the answer is a divine yes.

Why stop at ten righteous? Didn't Abraham dare to push God further?

Do righteous people have a certain saving quality? Are others blessed for their sakes? Or does God's common grace bless both without distinction (Matt. 5:44)? Explain your answer.

We tend to contrast divine justice and mercy. But Luther learned that it's God's *justice* that saves us! What does this passage from Genesis reveal about divine justice and mercy?

CHAPTER 13

ABRAHAM TESTED
Genesis 22:1-19

This difficult and problematic story begins with a sentence that gives us insight into the divine intention in what follows. We're given a glimpse into the councils of heaven (as in Gen. 1:26 and Job 1). God intends to manipulate Abraham, holding his feet to the fire, testing his faith. We, the readers, know this is a test; Abraham doesn't.

As you read this story, think about the earlier story of the calling of Abram (Gen. 12). That was the first time the divine voice spoke to him; this is the last. There are language echoes: "Go to the land I will show you," and now, "Go to . . . one of the mountains I will tell you about" (v. 2). Notice also that in 12:1 Abraham is commanded to leave three things: "your country, your people, and your father's household." That is balanced at the beginning of this story with the triple naming of Isaac. The first time God spoke to Abraham, God's words were a call to faith and obedience; this story tells of God's radical test of that faith.

The voice of God speaks to Abraham, calling his name. He gives a servant's answer, "Here am I," that is, "Yes, Sir." There is none of the amazing openness and intimacy Abraham experienced with God at Mamre, but rather a meeting of master and servant, a pattern of command and unquestioned obedience.

> **Satan tempts us (1 Cor. 7:5), but God tests us (James 1:13). What's the difference? Purpose? Endurance? Anything else? (See 1 Cor. 10:13.)**

A Cruel Mystery

Why did God order this? Why does God test us with death of a loved one, cancer, crippling, and other trials? Does it ever make sense to us?

Notice the three descriptions of Isaac. This is Abraham's son and heir. Since ten years earlier, when Sarah insisted that Abraham send Ishmael away (21:10), it was as if Isaac was Abraham's only son—the son whom he loved. All this makes the command that follows more poignant and difficult to understand. God orders Abraham to take this son, the child of the promise, and sacrifice him as a burnt offering on Mount Moriah.

Why did Abraham obey without question or protest? Why didn't he pray as Jesus did in Gethsemane? Or do you think he did? How would you have reacted?

Notice that the narrative offers no explanation for this outrageous command, or for why Abraham acquiesces. We know God is running a test. But Abraham doesn't know that. Early Jewish tradition objected strongly to this demand of God, since the Torah clearly forbids such child sacrifice (Lev. 18:21; 20:1-5; Deut. 18:10). Some speculate that in Abraham's time this might have been thought an appropriate way to worship God. But there is nothing to indicate that. Furthermore, this was the child through whom God's promise would be fulfilled.

Do you think he told Sarah? If not, why not? How do you think she would have reacted?

Still, Abraham is silent and obedient. Some early interpreters think he didn't even tell Sarah of God's command, for fear that she might try to persuade him to disobey. Others speculate that Sarah died of shock when she later heard about it.

The text relates the deliberate preparations that Abraham himself makes for this pilgrimage to the holy site. He cuts the wood, gathers his party, and sets out for Mount Moriah. Moriah is thought to be the location of the temple mount in Jerusalem and the present site of the Dome of the Rock. The amount of detail included in this story and the slow pace of the narrative increases our suspense. Will he or won't he?

God Provides

Are Abraham's words to the servants deliberately deceptive or does he really believe both will return (see Heb. 11:17-19)?

It's about fifty miles from Beersheba to Mt. Moriah. On the third day—in Hebrew usage this has the same sense of a crisis as does our English phrase "at the eleventh hour"—they see the mountain. Here Abraham leaves the servants and the donkey, going on alone with Isaac. Notice that he indicates to them that both will be coming back.

Does Abraham's reply to Isaac express faith or resignation?

Isaac is probably a teenage boy. He is strong enough to carry the firewood but still too young to distrust his father. Isaac asks an innocent question: "Where is the lamb for the burnt offering?" Notice the intimate "my father" and "my son" in this exchange. Abraham's reply is a pivotal point in the story, but an uncertain one. After all, God had provided Isaac through a long-delayed and miraculous birth. Is this what Abraham means? Or does he expect divine intervention? This question and answer significantly increase the tension that continues to build in the story.

Again we have a deliberate description, this time of Abraham's actual preparations for the sacrifice of Isaac. The Hebrew word for "sacrifice" here means "slaughter" and is used for child sacrifice in pagan cults (see Isa. 57:5; Ezek. 16:21). The binding is traditionally done to an animal about to be sacrificed. Notice we are told nothing of how Isaac might have reacted to this treatment.

How do you think Isaac reacted? Did he cooperate? Or did he fight being bound? How would you have reacted?

The voice of an angel interrupts Abraham, calling his name twice to express urgency. Again he gives the servant's response, "Here am I." Now comes the relief of the angel's instruction not to harm Isaac and a statement that shows that the test is completed and Abraham has passed. Now God "knows" that Abraham fears God, since Abraham is willing to sacrifice even his son—the son he not only loves but who is also the concrete sign of the divine promise.

Was this test intended to let God know for sure what was in Abraham's heart? How does that fit with divine omniscience? Or was this test for Abraham's sake? How do you interpret this?

Abraham's surprise at suddenly discovering the ram caught in the bushes reflects the extent of his emotional involvement in what has occurred. He takes the ram to be the sacrifice provided by God, in fulfillment of what he said earlier. So God the tester has become God the provider.

ABRAHAM BLESSED

The story closes with a powerful divine affirmation of the promise to bless Abraham and his descendants. This is appropriate, since Abraham has shown his willingness to forfeit all this in order to obey the divine command. The divine oath and the word "surely" (vv. 16-17) are the keys to this statement. The Lord commits himself absolutely to be the God of the people that will be born of Abraham. Notice again how the words of blessing reflect the initial blessing promised (12:2-3).

Here the stories about Abraham end, on this note of unflinching faith which makes this patriarch, in Paul's words, "the father of all believers" (Rom. 4:16-17).

How do you think this story fits in with the fact that Jesus becomes the substitute sacrifice for our sins?

CHAPTER 14

A WIFE FOR ISAAC
Genesis 24

The first verse of chapter 24 gives the impression that Abraham is arranging for a wife for Isaac because he feels himself to be near life's end. But jump ahead to the beginning of Chapter 25 and you discover that Abraham marries again, has six sons, and lives for probably another thirty-five years. So what's going on here?

The preceding chapter gives the clue. Sarah has died and the important role of mother of the covenant is vacant. So it is necessary to find a suitable bride for Isaac. Abraham's concern that this person not be a Canaanite goes beyond that of a father wanting his son to have a good wife. A Canaanite wife would worship other gods and hold other ideas of right and wrong. Abraham's absolute prohibition against Isaac leaving Canaan, the land of promise, shows his awareness of the covenant obligations that rest on Isaac and that will include this new wife also.

Notice the trust Abraham places in his chief servant, Eliezer of Damascus (Gen. 15:2). He seems to be a sort of trustee who is in charge of Abraham's estate until Isaac is old enough to take over that responsibility. Eliezer swears to find Isaac a proper wife. He does so by placing his hand under Abraham's thigh, evidently a gesture indicating the seriousness of the oath. Notice the name and description of God that

> **Why do you think Abraham objected to a Canaanite wife? Customs? Morals? Religion? How would you feel under similar circumstances?**

> **Why didn't Abraham send Isaac to find a wife for himself? Because he was too young (around forty, according to 25:20)? Because of his character (too inexperienced)? Because Isaac couldn't leave the land of Canaan? Or was the reason cultural (the father was responsible to find a bride for his son)?**

> **What do you think of Eliezer testing God in this way? Would it be proper for us to do something similar?**

> **Is hospitality still a virtue for Christians today? (See Rom. 12:13; 1 Tim. 3:2; 1 Pet. 4:9.)**

> **Should Christians also think of wealth as being a divine blessing? How does this fit with Jesus' statement, "Blessed are you who are poor" (Luke 6:20)?**

Abraham gives in verse 3. That shows us that Abraham does not, like the neighboring people, worship a God of the land, river, or sky. No! His God rules all heaven and earth.

TESTING GOD'S WILL

The rest of the chapter is a long, involved story of how Abraham's servant finds a proper wife for Isaac. The bride-finding stories in the Bible (Jacob meeting Rachel in Genesis 29, Moses meeting Zipporah in Exodus 2) all have some common elements. A stranger meets a woman at the well and draws water, thereby getting her attention and consequently receiving an introduction to her father. Probably in that day the village well was one of the few places where single women encountered men, even strangers. Like a shopping mall today, it was a prime gathering place.

The test that Eliezer devises and places before God is not an arbitrary one. He doesn't pray, "God, let the first woman wearing blue be the chosen one." It would be a considerable amount of work for the girl to give him a drink and then draw water also for his camels. Doing this would display a concern for strangers and a willingness to help the helpless with no prospect of reward—an unusual kindness for that day. It displayed hospitality similar to Abraham's—remember his kindness to the three men at Mamre (18:1-8). Most people were indifferent, even hostile, to strangers. So this was a test designed to find a girl who shared the moral values of Abraham's family. That quality of true hospitality is confirmed in the way Rebekah invites these strangers to spend the night at her father's house and by the welcome her brother Laban gives them.

The long section in which Eliezer reviews for Laban and Rebekah's family everything that has occurred earlier in this chapter (vv. 34-49) seems redundant. Why repeat all this? But this section gives a stately character to the narrative, turning this betrothal into a sort of formal treaty between two branches of the same clan. It emphasizes also the importance of the search. Eliezer, the conscientious servant, makes sure that everything is done decently and in good order.

Notice also how Eliezer emphasizes Abraham's wealth (vv. 22, 35, 53). In that culture wealth would be interpreted as a sign of divine approval and, on a human level, certainly would help to facilitate the betrothal. Laban seems to have the power in his family. He is clearly impressed by the expensive gifts and is quite willing to have his sister marry into this affluent family.

CHARACTERS

Finally, notice how deftly this little story sketches the characters of the main actors. You get a clear picture of the sort of person each of them was, what sort of faith they had, and whether you would have liked them or not.

Abraham is a giant of faith. He sees clearly what must be done and trusts God to help the servant bring back a suitable wife for Isaac. There seems to be no doubt in his mind that God will make this venture successful. Eliezer is conscientious and careful. He speaks of the Lord as "God of my master Abraham," but is wise in choosing a test that will reveal the right girl. He trusts that God will guide this entire matter. His mission dominates his actions; he will not even eat until he has told Laban about it.

Laban is a greedy, grasping person, mightily impressed by the wealth of great-uncle Abraham (vv. 30-31). Still, he and his father, Bethuel, show their faith by stating, "This is from the Lord" (v. 50). We are tempted to wonder whether Bethuel's faith is not stronger than Laban's. As we find out later in his dealings with Jacob, Laban is a very cunning and unreliable person (Gen. 30).

Isaac has little active part in this story. Only at the very end does he come into the picture. This fits with the character of Isaac, clearly the most passive of all the patriarchs.

Rebekah, on the other hand, turns out to be the most active and forceful of all the matriarchs. That is clear already in this story and becomes even clearer in her later dealings with her husband and sons. She is ready to invite these strangers into her father's house and to leave immediately with them to travel to Canaan. She is a very courageous and decisive young woman. Leaving home and family for an unknown husband and future is no easy step. Rebekah takes it unhesitatingly.

Nowhere in this story does God speak. The Lord is silent. Yet, as we read, we get a strong sense of the divine presence. The strong, active faith of the persons in the story leaves us without any doubt that God is controlling and directing everything that occurs. God has provided this wife for Isaac and this new mother of the covenant family. God continues to lead and guide his chosen people.

Which of the main characters in this story do you admire or like the most? The least?

Consider what you have learned from this story—about finding a wife or husband, about testing God, about the courage of faith, about the ways in which God guides us in this life.

CHAPTER 15

STRUGGLE FOR THE BLESSING
Genesis 25:19-34; 27

Genesis is full of stories about rivalry between brothers. That was a basic fact of life in those days of primogeniture, when the eldest inherited the most property and the right to rule over younger siblings. In Genesis this rigid human custom is disrupted by divine election, as, again and again, God chooses the younger and weaker. In this story the struggle with his brother, Esau, dominates the entire first half of Jacob's life.

Have you experienced such rivalry in your family? What form did it take? How was it resolved?

TWINS AT ODDS

This rivalry, we are told, began already in the womb—much to Rebekah's distress (25:22ff.). The oracle from the Lord (in typical poetic form) predicts two nations in conflict and that the younger will be victorious. This prediction sets the tensions of the plot in motion but leaves open the question of precisely how this oracle will be fulfilled. Will it be done by divine or human action?

Do you think Rebekah told the boys about the oracle? What effect might it have had on them?

After their birth these twins are described as contrasting personalities, in their appearance as well as in their actions. Such physical descriptions are highly unusual in the Bible, so we know that the narrator considers them important to the story. Esau is "red" (robust, direct, passionate) and "hairy"

How do you suppose Jacob felt about being condemned to be the lesser, subject son, even though he and Esau were born just minutes apart?

(masculine, uncouth). He becomes a hunter, seen in Bible times as a low calling. Jacob is "grasping" and "smooth" (slick, deceptive—see 27:11). He prefers the tents. Jacob is also described as "a quiet man" (25:27). This Hebrew word means "innocent," "upright," "orderly." It seems to be in contrast to Esau's wild character. To make things worse, the parents—themselves contrasting personalities—each favor a different son. So the stage is set for trouble!

The story about the bartered birthright (the double inheritance for the eldest son) brings out the contrasts even more sharply. Notice that Esau is crude of speech and impatient to satisfy his bodily desires. Jacob thinks of the future and can wait. After the deal is struck, the description of Esau's actions is striking: "He ate and drank, and then got up and left" (25:34). In other words, he gulped down his food and promptly forgot about it.

In a story remarkable for its lack of moral judgment about the actions taken in it, the very last sentence of this chapter becomes a crucial condemnation of Esau. He despised his birthright. What was vitally important to the family and the tribe wasn't worth the price of a bowl of chili at a fast food joint to Esau.

ALL IN THE FAMILY

The next part of the story about this dysfunctional family takes place more than forty years later (26:34). It's ironic that the struggle is over the blessing, both patriarchal and divine. But the actions, at least Rebekah's and Jacob's, are full of lies and deception. Notice that the fact that Jacob wins the blessing by trickery doesn't seem to bother the narrator. For us it raises serious questions. Could it be that the immorality was so clear to the Jewish readers that this didn't even need to be mentioned? Or is moral judgment on Jacob's actions expressed in more subtle ways in later stories?

Notice that with the second verse the story switches to direct discourse, giving us insights into the feelings and purposes of the four participants.

Isaac emerges as the patriarch who sets his house in order before he dies. That he doesn't actually die until many years later (when he is 180—see 35:28-29) is irrelevant to the story. A meal often accompanied the parental blessing, but what is noted here is Isaac's desire for a dish of wild game. This food was also the reason why he loved Esau (25:28).

Which of the two, Jacob of Esau, would you prefer as a friend? Why? Who do you think the early Jewish readers preferred? The New Testament writers (see Heb. 12:16)?

Is it better to want the right things and go about getting them in the wrong way (Jacob) or not to want the right things at all (Esau)? Why?

In this part of the story, who wins your sympathy? Why? Would an Old Testament reader feel the same?

Esau is presented as the dutiful son doing just what his father asks. Also, surprisingly, toward the end of the story he is presented as someone who desperately desires his father's blessing. He pleads for "only one blessing, my father" (27:38). One can't help but feel sorry for Esau.

Rebekah comes through as the strongest character of the four. She's the one who hatches the plot, persuades Jacob to go along with it, answers all his objections, and is even willing to take upon herself any curse Isaac may utter if he learns that he has been deceived. There is a decidedly ruthless streak in this woman.

Jacob appears to be nervous about this deception. Not that he has qualms about deceiving his father! He wants the blessing too much to worry about that. But he fears that his father will discover the plot and give him a curse instead of a blessing. Jacob is revealed as an ambitious, self-serving man, lacking in sympathy for either his father or his brother.

If Rebekah and Jacob believed the oracle, why did they resort to deceit to try to make it come true?

THE BLESSING

At the center of the story lies the blessing. The entire family is preoccupied with it. They all believe that this blessing has the power to determine the future. To us that is a strange notion. But recognize that this is a merging of the traditional parental blessing and the divine blessing promised to Abraham. The blessing has become the reason for this family's existence and its hope for the future. According to the words of Isaac, it can provide unqualified fertility, well-being, and political power.

The final irony of this story is that after all this trickery, Jacob seems to have gained nothing. He must run for his life because Esau is determined to kill him. Then, when this fugitive sleeps with a stone for his pillow on the road to Paddam Aram, God appears to him in a dream and gives him freely everything that he has worked so hard to wrest from Esau (28:12-15). Why didn't he just wait and pray to God for the privilege of bearing the blessing? Clearly it was not his to win or own anyway. It could come to him only as the Lord's gracious gift.

Does this almost magical notion of the blessing (and the curse) seem inappropriate to you? How does it fit with what you know about God and the Old Testament people?

This story clearly doesn't teach good morals. So what does it teach? Divine faithfulness? How God disrupts our social systems? Or how God uses ambiguous human motives to accomplish divine purposes?

67

CHAPTER 16

GOD BLESSES JACOB
Genesis 29:14b-30:43

To read properly the story of Jacob's labors with Laban, we need to recognize two things. First, notice that this is a Horatio Alger type of story in which a young man goes from rags to riches. Jacob arrives at Paddam Aram with nothing more than the clothes on his back. He leaves twenty years later with a vast accumulation of wealth: wives, children, camels, donkeys, livestock, and servants. This transition from poverty to wealth provides living proof of the effectiveness of both Isaac's blessing and the Lord's promise at Bethel: "I am with you and will watch over you wherever you go . . ." (28:15).

Second, we need to read this as a story full of irony and humor. Hearing this tale, the ancient Jews probably roared with laughter over its funny twists and turns as Jacob (the great deceiver) is deceived, and Laban (the consummate cheater) is cheated. To fully appreciate the biblical narratives, we sometimes need to laugh along with them.

THE DECEIVER DECEIVED

After the meeting at the well, Jacob is welcomed into Laban's family as a nephew. But that doesn't last long. A relative was not paid wages. So Laban challenges the long-term validity of continuing their relationship on that basis. Jacob agrees. But

Horatio Alger tales emphasize the personal qualities of thrift and hard work. The stories about Jacob emphasize divine blessing. Which is more accurate? Are both needed?

Some people think humor is inappropriate in the Bible or in a sermon. Do you agree? Why is it included here? Can you give other examples of humor in the Bible?

by accepting wages, Jacob becomes an indentured servant. Laban is now his master. Notice how the word *serve* occurs again and again throughout the narrative. This is ironic. After Jacob risked so much to gain the blessing so that he could avoid serving Esau, he ends up serving Laban instead.

Why does Jacob agree? Because he's already in love with Rachel, but he can't afford to pay the bride price. Notice, however, Laban's reply to Jacob's proposal. He says, "It's better I give her to you than to some other man" (29:19). Rachel isn't named. Laban may already be thinking of Leah as the bride he will give to Jacob.

It's difficult to know what to make of Leah's "weak eyes" (29:17). It's obviously mentioned in contrast to Rachel's beauty. The word for "weak" can mean "delicate," or "youthful." Probably, at a time when lustrous eyes peeping over a veil were considered a prime criterion of beauty, Leah's eyes lacked sparkle.

> Do you think Leah and Rachel were willing partners in this deception, or were they forced to cooperate?

After seven years of work Jacob asks for the marriage with "his wife" to be consummated. Laban doesn't answer him directly but does hold a wedding feast. However, he sneaks Leah into the bridal bed instead of Rachel. The bride is heavily veiled (compare with 24:65), the room dark, and the groom probably drunk. Those factors all combine to make the trick possible. So Jacob, who deceived his own blind father, is now deceived in turn.

> Like Laban, do we use custom to justify dishonesty? When?

Notice that Laban doesn't apologize in answer to Jacob's accusations. He seems surprised by Jacob's outrage and rebukes him. To marry off the younger daughter first would have been a serious violation of custom, Laban insists. So the law of primogeniture has stung Jacob again. Still, he is also given Rachel as his wife, although she'll cost him another seven years of labor.

More Rivalry

The next ironic twist to the story is the fierce competition between the sisters/wives, which reflects the earlier competition between the brothers. This time it's not over an inheritance but over children and social status. The root cause is that Jacob favors Rachel, echoing the earlier favoritism shown by Isaac and Rebekah. Children seem to repeat their parents' mistakes.

> Does God always favor people, like Leah, who are mistreated? Is this a consistent biblical theme? Consider the prophets and the Beatitudes.

Now the Lord steps in. Because Leah is evidently unloved, God lets her become pregnant while Rachel stays barren. After Leah has four sons, Rachel turns on Jacob in envy and despair, blaming him for her lack of children. Jacob answers with a rhetorical question that is really a dismissive rebuke (29:1-2). So now there's trouble between them also.

The struggle continues. Each of the wives uses her personal maid as a surrogate mother. After two sons are born to each, we have the story of the mandrake—a tomato-like fruit that was believed to be an aphrodisiac. Leah receives two more sons and a daughter. But finally God intervenes again, and Rachel has her son. Her disgrace is taken away, and the tension eases.

Does a childless wife still face the same ignominy she would have experienced in biblical times? How has that changed? What is the core issue, if any, today?

Ill-Gotten Gain?

Next the story turns to Jacob's successful efforts to gain property. He asks his master to let him leave (30:25). But Laban realizes that God is making him rich because of Jacob. The blessing is spilling over (12:3).

The deal they strike for wages seems to favor Laban because sheep of that region were usually white, while goats were black. Only twenty percent or less were irregular—speckled or spotted. Laban separates the latter to make sure they don't interbreed.

But Jacob is even more clever. He uses primitive breeding methods—ones that don't make a lot of sense to us—to increase the number of speckled and spotted sheep.

The result of all this maneuvering and conniving is that much of Laban's newly gained wealth is transferred to Jacob. This result is so pronounced that Laban's sons accuse Jacob of taking "everything our father owned" (31:1). But, as Jacob explains to his wives, what has really happened is that "God has taken away your father's livestock and has given them to me" (31:9).

We find in Jacob a remarkable mixture of human cleverness and faith in God's providing. He trusts God, but he is never passive. He always looks for any little advantage in dealing with others. His is a striving faith.

Are there various kinds of faith, such as a waiting faith, a knowing faith, a praising faith, a striving faith, and so on? If so, what kind do you have? What kind do you consider best?

CHAPTER 17

THE BROTHERS MEET
Genesis 32-33

To understand this story, we must appreciate Jacob's dilemma. God ordered him to "Go back to the land of your fathers and to your relatives, and I will be with you" (31:3). But Esau, one of those relatives, has sworn to kill Jacob. So Jacob enters fearfully into Canaan. The slow pace of the story increases our feelings of foreboding. Any misstep could be fatal.

Notice the recurring themes of messengers and meetings. On the way Jacob is met by mysterious messengers from God. They are strangely silent—messengers without a message—but they seem to promise protection. One of Jacob's first acts is to send messengers to his brother, inviting a meeting. Then Jacob meets a man who wrestles with him. Eventually he meets Esau. Clearly something fateful is occurring between God and Jacob and between Esau and Jacob.

FACE TO FACE WITH THE PAST
The messengers that Jacob sends would have followed the custom of that day by telling Esau, "Thus says your servant Jacob. . . . " Then they would give Jacob's words verbatim. Notice the humble language "my lord Esau" and "your servant Jacob." The twenty-year absence is glossed over and the

What would you think if a letter from one of your siblings used such humble language? How do you think Esau reacted?

73

> **How would you have interpreted Esau's response—heading your way with four hundred armed men and not a single word in answer to your overtures for peace? Do you think Esau actually intended to attack Jacob but later changed his mind? What other reasons might there have been for his response?**

> **Evaluate Jacob's mixture of planning and prayer. Was he just being smart? Or did his conniving indicate that he lacked faith? How do we know when we should act and when we should wait for God to act?**

> **Who is this man? A demon who guards the ford at night? God in human form? An angel (see Hosea 12:4)? Why does he dislocate Jacob's hip socket? To avoid defeat? As a reminder? To humble Jacob?**

> **Once all Christians received new names at baptism; in some places that's still done. Why don't we follow this custom? Does a new name encourage a new nature?**

message highlights the surprising wealth of Jacob and his desire to gain Esau's favor.

Esau answers not a word but sets out to meet Jacob with four hundred men—the standard size of a militia group (see 1 Sam. 22:2). That's threatening, and Jacob is appropriately frightened. Typically, he responds by mixing calculation and faith, planning and prayer.

First Jacob divides his people into two groups. That way, while Esau attacks one group, the other may perhaps escape. Next Jacob prays to God, including every basis on which he might ask for divine favor. He asks for divine deliverance from Esau: "Save me, I pray, from the hand of my brother. . . ." He also sends substantial gifts ahead to Esau. The message he sends along with each of them is intended to pacify Esau.

Jacob's gift to Esau should also be understood as an implicit admission of guilt. By conning Esau out of the birthright and stealing the blessing, he had taken worldly goods away. Now he gives them back. This way he confesses that he did wrong. That is also the way he expects Esau to understand the gift.

God-Wrestler

Next we encounter a mysterious interlude as Jacob remains alone on the shore of the Jabbock, probably to think and plan. There a man—that's all the text says about this person—attacks him. They wrestle in a deadly encounter. But Jacob is strong enough to resist the man until the stranger touches and wrenches the socket of his hip. Even then Jacob holds him in a grip that the man cannot break.

We aren't told why this man does not want to be seen in daylight—something that has caused much speculation. Whatever the reason, the request evidently makes Jacob suspect that this is more than an ordinary human. So he demands a blessing. The man's response is first to rename him "Israel" (literally, "God will strive"), probably meaning "God-wrestler." When Jacob humbly asks his name in return, the man says, in effect, "Jacob, don't you realize who I am?" He then blesses Jacob.

This incident is a major turning point in Jacob's personal history. The important name change makes that clear. He had been the deceiver, the tricky one, and was so named. Now, with the new name, he receives a new nature, that of God-wrestler. He still strives, but now in a vastly different way.

That difference is shown in his confident meeting with Esau. Jacob divides his family into three groups in inverse order of their value to him. But he himself goes first to meet his brother.

Notice the marked difference in the behavior of these two brothers. Esau greets Jacob as a loving brother, embracing him, asking natural questions, ready to keep him company, inviting him to come and live in Seir. Jacob is formal and distant, bowing seven times, addressing Esau as "my lord," and clearly wanting to put some distance between them by politely refusing to be traveling companions and by settling in a different area.

The impression that the text gives is that past conflicts and the wrong that Jacob has done his brother have remained as heavy weights on his conscience. He can't just dismiss them even though Esau has clearly forgiven him. He can't be a loving brother. Esau, on the other hand, has long forgotten his anger and his brother's misdeeds.

Is this just a difference of character? Or is the one wronged able to forgive and forget better than the one who wrongs? Think of examples from your personal experience.

It's ironic that, after the struggle over the blessing, both have plenty of riches (33:9). Still, Jacob insists that his brother accept the gift offered. For him it's an important symbol. Esau accepts it because it would be discourteous for him to continue to refuse. He sees how important it is to Jacob for him to do so.

So Jacob and Esau have met and are now reconciled. Their personal conflict, as predicted by the oracle, had been the ruling motif in their relationship. It is now ended, although it will erupt again between their descendants. Jacob settles in Canaan near the city of Shechem. Life begins its normal rhythm, as this God-wrestler pitches his tent, builds an altar, and worships his Lord.

Instead of struggling with his brother, was Jacob actually wrestling with God all along? Was it at the Jabbock that he finally realized it? Is that true in our own lives as well? Where do you see this kind of wrestling in your own life?

CHAPTER 18

JOSEPH THE DREAMER
Genesis 37

The remainder of the book of Genesis presents the Joseph cycle of stories. These serve as a transition from the chosen people's patriarchal years in Canaan to their slavery years in Egypt. Jacob has settled in Canaan. That is in contrast to his ancestors, who had lived there as sojourners (37:1). He seems to have lost the sense of being a pilgrim in the land. That makes the move to Egypt necessary.

Notice that from here to the end of the book there is a markedly different way of talking about God. There are no more divine voices, appearances, and visions. God speaks only through cryptic dreams. The divine purposes work in hidden, unnoticed, though still reliable, ways.

Notice the similiarities between the Joseph stories and the ones about Daniel—dreams, interpretations of dreams, a remarkable young man in a foreign land, and so on. What do you make of this?

IN HIS DREAMS

Obviously this is not a happy family; the relationship between Joseph and his brothers isn't a good one. According to the story, the fault for this lies with Joseph himself and with Jacob. Joseph tells his father tales about the misbehavior of his brothers, the four sons of the concubines. And Jacob shows his obvious preference for this son of his old age and of his favored wife, Rachel, by giving him a robe worthy of a young prince. That gives Joseph higher status in the family and

Why hadn't Jacob learned the dangers of favoritism? Character too set? Feelings too deep?

inspires his brothers' hatred. So we have a father who plays favorites and a spoiled, proud teenager.

Injected into this highly unstable situation are Joseph's dreams. Notice the parallel here to the oracle in the Jacob story. Both oracles provide insight into the trouble that follows, but they also provoke it. God seems to be making an already bad situation worse. Notice also how paired dreams run through this story: the dreams of Joseph, the jailed servants, and Pharaoh all come in twos.

Why does Joseph receive these dreams? To warn that God is at work? To hint at God's mysterious ways? To challenge faith?

In those days it was assumed that a dream was a message from God given in symbols, not words. But dreams were also understood to express the hidden needs and wishes of the dreamer. So first Joseph's brothers and then his father quickly interpret these dreams as expressions of Joseph's desire to reign over them. None of them take kindly to the arrogance of this wish, but the brothers respond with hatred and jealousy while Jacob offers only a mild rebuke and thinks deeply about the dream.

What do you think of young Joseph? Likable? An arrogant brat? A lonely teenager?

It should strike you how guileless and socially naive Joseph appears to be in telling his family about these dreams. His manner, as well as the dream contents, must have been offensive. Remember that at this stage he's only an unsophisticated young boy.

THE NIGHTMARE BEGINS

Why did Jacob send Joseph to check up on his brothers? Didn't he realize the depth of their hatred? Was he just naive?

The second part of this story begins with Jacob sending Joseph to check on his brothers' well-being (or *shalom*). This is ironic since the text said earlier that the brothers were not able to speak peaceably ("with shalom") to Joseph because of their hatred (37:4). Joseph goes on a fifty-mile solitary trek to Shechem and after that he travels another sixty-five miles to Dothan before he meets up with them.

What do you make of this stranger who gives Joseph directions? Why do you suppose this incident is included in the text?

Notice the interlude about "a man" who meets Joseph and directs him on to where his brothers are grazing the sheep. The fact that this little incident is included points to its having some special significance. Perhaps this is a guide sent by God, although there is no revelatory word spoken here.

When Joseph's ten brothers see him approaching, they immediately plan to kill this "master dreamer," as they sarcastically name him. The text gives the impression that they all quickly agree on this action, except for the eldest, Reuben, who persuades them just to throw Joseph in a cistern. Reuben intends to rescue him later.

These cisterns were dug from the rock and shaped like jars. It was impossible for anyone to climb out unassisted. They were commonly used to imprison criminals or to dispose of bodies.

What happens next? Some think we have a combination of two earlier versions of the story. The reasons for this are the designations of the traders as "Ishmaelites" (v. 25) and as "Midianites" (v. 28), as well as the cryptic "they" who pulled Joseph out of the cistern (v. 28—the NIV translates this "the brothers" but the Hebrew text does not have that addition).

So in one original version of this story, Joseph is left in the pit. Passing Midianite traders hear his cries, pull him out, and sell him as a slave (vv. 24-28, 29; see also 40:15). In the other version Judah suggests they sell Joseph to the Ishmaelites for twenty pieces of silver (vv. 25-27, 28b; according to Lev. 27:5 this was the going rate for a young slave).

The writer may have deftly combined these two earlier versions of the story to show the roles of both Reuben and Judah. Or this may always have been one story. Judah may have suggested the sale to get around Reuben's objections to killing the boy and also to make a little money from the transaction. Reuben's role is admirable; Judah's is not.

Notice that there isn't a single word about Joseph's reaction to this brutal treatment from his brothers, although later they talk guiltily about how he pleaded for his life (42:21). We need to remember that the biblical text omits what the author considers irrelevant to the point of the story.

Technically, the brothers don't lie to their father. They bring back the blood-stained robe and just say, "We found this" (v. 32). They let Jacob draw the conclusion that Joseph must have been killed by a wild animal. There is a final irony in that Jacob, who deceives his father with the skin of a kid, is himself deceived by the blood of a goat.

The story closes with a description of Jacob's deep sorrow, which he resolves to carry with him to the grave. Meanwhile Joseph is brought to Egypt, where he is sold as a slave to serve in the house of Potiphar.

What do you think of this theory of two original versions? Does it take away from the truthfulness of the Word? Or does it just add an insight into the origins of this story? Why?

So what is the point of this story? How does it speak to you personally?

Chapter 19

Joseph the Slave
Genesis 39; 41:1-46

The second segment of the Joseph stories is a masterfully written account that covers the twelve years from the time that Joseph was sold as a slave to the time of his being appointed prime minister of the entire Egyptian empire. It's important to note the repetition in this story since it is crafted, like a musical composition, into a central theme with a number of variations.

If God Is With Us . . .

Simply stated, the theme of this section is "The Lord was with Joseph and . . . gave him success in everything he did" (39:2-3).

That theme is elaborated in the succeeding verses (vv. 3-6). Notice the repeated use of "everything," "anything," and "all." The blessing of God, centered in this young slave, bubbles over, as it were. It makes everything and everybody around Joseph prosper also. Even his owner, Potiphar, sees this as the hand of the Lord (39:2) and entrusts his whole household to Joseph's care.

The next variation on this theme comes when Joseph is put in prison. The warden sees his ability and puts everything in his care (vv. 21-23). The culminating variation occurs

> **How do you relate God's "being with Joseph" to Jesus' promise to "be with us always" (Matt. 28:20)?**
>
> **How did Potiphar know that the Lord was with Joseph (v. 3)?**

when Joseph counsels Pharaoh and is placed in charge of the entire land of Egypt (41:41, 44).

How are we to understand this theme? Are we to see Joseph as a master administrator and planner who is personable, dashingly handsome, absolutely trustworthy, and an excellent speaker even though he learned Egyptian as a late teen? Or should we see Joseph as a pawn of God, passive and weak in and of himself—someone who is successful only because of the divine blessing?

Remember that human gifts and abilities also come from God. God undoubtedly gifted Joseph with some unusual abilities and skills. But for a slave that wouldn't be enough. So at crucial points, God tips the scales in Joseph's favor. The inscrutable power of God assists him through many lonely and miserable years.

UNJUST TREATMENT OF THE JUST

Rarely does the Bible give a physical description of someone. Calling Joseph handsome hints at the trouble that starts when Potiphar's wife bluntly propositions him. Notice the contrast. She uses just a few words, but Joseph is voluble in giving practical reasons why he refuses her. As slave mistress, she is used to giving blunt orders. As a slave, Joseph is defensive, knowing the extreme danger of denying his mistress anything.

When Potiphar's wife turns aggressive, Joseph runs away. Perhaps his flight is witnessed by someone in the household, so she must manufacture a defense. Or perhaps she just wants revenge. At any rate, she makes a cunning accusation. Notice how she plays on the possible resentment the other household slaves might feel towards Joseph because of his superior position over them. She speaks of "this Hebrew" who insults the household (39:14). Notice also the subtle changes in what she tells Potiphar. Joseph's cloak is beside her, where he would leave it after disrobing. It's no longer in her hand as a result of her grabbing it. Also, she claims she "screamed for help" as a virtuous wife would do (39:18).

Potiphar is understandably angry and puts Joseph in prison. This is probably a building located on Potiphar's estate and under his control as captain of the guard. So Joseph has fallen even lower in status than a mere slave. But again the Lord is with him, and he lands on his feet. Soon he's placed in charge of the entire prison.

If God blesses a person, then that person will succeed. Does it follow that, if a person succeeds, God must be blessing and approving of that person?

How much of Joseph's refusal was prudence and how much was faith? Compare Proverbs 6:23-26 and 6:32-35. If we know something is a sin, do we need to look for other reasons not to do it?

If Potiphar was so angry, why do you suppose he didn't kill Joseph? Because he liked him? Because he doubted his wife's story? Another reason? What might Joseph have said in his own defense?

SAVING DREAMS

The story of Joseph's dealings with Pharaoh's cupbearer and baker proves him to be a skilled dream interpreter (by God's gift). It provides a later channel to Pharaoh. Notice Joseph's statement that "interpretations belong to God" (40:8).

Pharaoh has two dreams, the second doubling and confirming the first. Joseph later speaks of one dream (41:25) since the message is singular. The Nile, source of life and food in Egypt, has a prominent place in the first dream. The seven unhealthy cows and heads of grain swallowing up the healthy ones must have seemed threatening to Pharaoh. So he is troubled by the dreams and dissatisfied with the interpretations offered by his court experts.

When Joseph is summoned on recommendation of the cupbearer, he shows extraordinary confidence in promising Pharaoh that "God will give Pharaoh the answer he desires" (41:16). Pharaoh retells the dream, this time adding more intense descriptions of the unhealthy cows and grain. Joseph immediately interprets the dream as a parable, foretelling seven years of abundance followed by seven years of famine. It takes a brave man to openly announce such a message of woe. But evidently this dovetails with Pharaoh's own perceptions of the meaning of his dreams.

Then, with extraordinary presumption for a slave prisoner, Joseph advises Pharaoh on what he should do. He suggests a complete plan for dealing with the anticipated time of famine. When this is quickly approved by all his officials, Pharaoh sees Joseph himself as a "discerning and wise man" (41:33) and puts him "in charge of the whole land of Egypt" (41:41). For a third time the Lord is with Joseph and gives him success.

Notice the unusual description Pharaoh gives of Joseph as "one in whom is the spirit of God" (41:38). Worshiping a nature god, Pharaoh only means by this that Joseph seems to be divinely gifted, possessing skills and abilities beyond the ordinary human range.

The God-given ability to interpret dreams has given Joseph a hearing in Pharaoh's court. But it is his ability to plan and manage matters—equally God-given—that wins him royal favor and the high place he comes to occupy.

Considering their differing beliefs, how could Joseph speak so freely to Pharaoh about God and what God would do? Could you do that if you were talking with a Hindu or a Muslim?

How would you describe Joseph's faith? How does his faith differ from Abraham's? From Jacob's? Is there an added moral quality? In what ways might Joseph's faith be more like Daniel's?

Chapter 20

Joseph and His Brothers
Genesis 42; 44:18-45:15

This is a long, complex story that stretches over four chapters. It relates how Joseph meets his ten brothers again and is finally reconciled with them. It's best to read the entire story, but here we will concentrate on the sections cited above.

Joseph unmistakably dominates the account. He comes across as the one who knows, recognizes, and understands what is going on. He is even able to tell his brothers God's purpose in all that has occurred (45:5-7). By contrast, the brothers don't recognize Joseph and have no idea what's really happening. But Joseph's motives for acting as he does aren't clear. Why does he hide from his brothers, accuse them, imprison them, trick them, and scare them out of their wits? Is he fulfilling the dream, punishing them, testing them, or teaching them a lesson? Typical of biblical narrative, the text is ambiguous. All these motives appear to be present.

What do you think is Joseph's primary motive in his rough treatment of his brothers? Is it difficult to settle on a single one?

A Deliberate Misunderstanding

The story begins with Joseph's family facing starvation. But instead of acting to save the family, the brothers "just keep looking at each other" (42:1). This odd phrase seems to prefigure what they will be doing a lot of later in the story. Jacob

> **How do you think Joseph felt when he first saw his brothers? Angry? Lonely? Did he have mixed feelings? Why does he speak so harshly to them?**

tells them to get moving to Egypt. Notice they are all expendable except Benjamin. Yet this new favoritism doesn't seem to trigger the old, bitter hatred.

In Canaan they face an autocratic Egyptian but don't recognize him as their brother. Imagine the shock to Joseph to suddenly see his brothers appear, bowing before him as the dream had foretold. But he acts as if he doesn't know them or understand their language. He speaks to them through an interpreter.

Several times Joseph repeats his harsh accusation that they are spies. That throws them into a panic and triggers desperate protests from them that they are honest men, sons of one father, with another brother still in Canaan. Joseph promptly uses that last detail as a test of their honesty. He decides to throw them all in prison just as they had imprisoned him. They'll stay there until one of them can bring Benjamin back to Egypt.

> **Why did Joseph change his mind and send back all his brothers but one? Out of concern for the starving families? Out of concern for Jacob? Or to help convince Jacob to let Benjamin come with them?**

Three days later Joseph changes his mind and sends them all back except for Simeon. He still insists that they bring Benjamin to Egypt. The brothers see this as a divine punishment for the way they had treated Joseph, and Reuben adds a blaming "I told you so." Hearing this, Joseph is moved to tears.

A DOUBLE BIND

On the way back, one of the brothers discovers his money in his sack (42:27-28), and later they all find their money returned to them (42:35). This frightens and disheartens them. They had protested to the Egyptian lord that they were honest men, but this makes them look like thieves. Beyond that, this money forces a deeper recognition of their own guilt. Guilt over how they had treated Joseph is clearly expressed in their question, "What is this that God has done to us?" (v. 28). The money reminds them of the silver they were paid for selling him off as a slave.

> **Why did Joseph return their money? To test their honesty? To deepen their problems? Or to remind them of the money paid for selling Joseph?**

The money and their fright about it evidently help Jacob finally understand that the brothers were responsible for Joseph's disappearance twenty years earlier. He accuses them directly, "You have deprived me of my children" (42:36). Reuben's reply is singularly inappropriate.

> **Guilt haunts the brothers. They see each misfortune as a divine punishment. Do you find that's true for you as well? In what situations have you been tempted to view tragedies and misfortunes as God's judgments?**

The next chapter tells of the quandary that the brothers face. They need food, but they can't return without Benjamin. But Jacob had once entrusted Joseph to them and lost him. Now he fears that the same thing will happen with Rachel's other son. Judah finally persuades him (43:8ff.), and, with resignation (43:14), their father finally lets Benjamin go along. The second meeting with Joseph seems to go much better, but this time not only is the silver returned but Joseph's cup is hidden in Benjamin's sack. So they face Joseph again, once more under the threat of slavery.

TESTED

Joseph seems to have maneuvered them into the key test. They sold one of Rachel's children as a slave. Now he places them in a situation where they seem to have no choice but to leave the other one in slavery as well. Reading the story, one gets the impression that this is the question that has been haunting Joseph all along. Will the brothers betray a second of Rachel's children, or have they changed?

Behind this lies a deeper question. Until now the promise of God had been passed on to one child. Are all twelve now worthy to share in the promise? Or will it be limited again, this time to Joseph's line?

In Judah's speech—the longest in Genesis—notice his repeated use of the words "servant" (ten times), "my lord" (six times), and "father" (thirteen times). He expresses genuine love and concern for Jacob and no animosity toward Benjamin (the favorite). He ends by offering himself as a slave in the boy's place. This seems not to be the same Judah who cynically suggested they sell Joseph as a slave and so avoid any blood guilt. He and his brothers have passed Joseph's test. The bitter rivalry between the sons of Rachel and Leah is gone. And they have gained a new sensitivity and moral character.

Joseph responds by dropping his masquerade and revealing himself to his brothers. Notice that this only terrifies them. Joseph has come to understand that God has arranged all this " . . . to save your lives by a great deliverance" (45:7). When he finally convinces them of this fact, their fear is removed and they are able to talk with him as brothers. They are finally reconciled.

How do you think Benjamin felt through all of this? Afraid to go with his brothers? Eager to explore Egypt?

In the New Testament, people are changed by the Spirit's working. How were they changed in the Old Testament? By divine promises? By trials God sent? Which other Old Testament characters show a true change of heart?

Joseph came to see his life as a small part of God's working in human history. Are you able to do the same in your own life? What might God be accomplishing through you?